GOD'S
PEOPLE
TRIUMPHANT
in
PERILOUS
TIMES

GOD'S PEOPLE TRIUMPHANT in PERILOUS TIMES

BY FRANK DAMAZIO

God's People Triumphant in Perilous Times
Copyright © 1992 Frank Damazio
Eugene, Oregon 97401

ISBN 0-914936-79-4

Printed in the United States of America

DEDICATION

I would like to dedicate this book to the people of Eugene Christian Fellowship who have made pastoring and preaching a joy. Thank you for allowing a young pastor to have room to grow. Our 11 ½ years together hold precious memories.

FOREWORD

Few Christian People today are ignorant of the fact that our society is in the process of a radical change. In fact things around us are changing so rapidly that some are becoming frightened. In such times despair can even set in. But Frank Damazio does not think it needs to. This book, like few others, allows us to see our chaotic world from the perspective of the Kingdom of God and gives us the guidelines we need to relate to it in a way that pleases our Lord.

God's People Triumphant in Perilous Times is an outstanding book for at least five reasons:

1. It is based on the Bible. On page after page relevant scripture texts are printed out in full, right in the spots where they can be read and applied. I agree that it is important to allow the Word of God to guide us as we understand our role in the church and in society.

2. It is rooted in history. Frank Damazio helps us to get a long-range perspective on where we are now, by tracing where we have come from. He very perceptively analyzes the changes which have taken the New Testament church through the dark ages, through the Reformation, and into our twentieth century.

3. It is centralized in the church. Jesus said, "I will build my church." and this book is geared toward that very process. In a day when many people are disdainful of the church, Damazio helps us to see that God wants to restore His church and empower it to be out at the cutting edge of all that the Lord desires to do among us.

4. It is tuned in to the real world. With spiritual insight, Frank Damazio highlights the features of today's society which are relevant to our Christian life and witness. For example, he rightly sees that one of the most dangerous strongholds of evil is the rapidly rising New Age Movement, and he provides practical handles on how to deal with it.

5. It is sensitive to the Holy Spirit. Jesus says, "He that has an ear, let him hear what the Spirit is saying to the churches." Frank Damazio has this kind of an ear, He helps us open ourselves to hearing the authentic voice of God both directly and through prophetic ministries so that our activities can synchronize with God's desires. He, along with many others, emphasizes our basic need for humility, repentance, and righteousness if we are going to make any significance difference for God in today's society.

I know that this book will be as much of a treat for you as it was for me. It pulls no punches, but it is a book permeated with faith, it helps us believe that through God's power we can be a triumphant church and a triumphant people in these perilous times.

C. Peter Wagner
Fuller Theological Seminary

Pasadena, California

CONTENTS

1

Twelve Perilous Present Day Conditions

"These could be great days of revival and influence for God's people or terrible days of defeat and disillusionment."

God's People Triumphant in Perilous Times is not only the title of this book, but the true predicament we find ourselves in as the people of God. The Bible speaks of the many pressures that will fall upon the church prior to the coming of Christ. Perilous times are here. What will be the extent of these perilous times? How can we as the people of God prepare ourselves to live triumphantly in such times as these?

Before God's people will prepare for perilous times they must believe we are in perilous times now. The church must be awakened to the fact that we are in a spiritual crisis. It is amazing, but it seems that most Christians do not perceive the church to be in what could be one of the most severe spiritual struggles it has ever

1

faced. Perhaps preachers of doom and gloom do not fit the present state of the church which would like to "eat, drink, and be merry for tomorrow we're raptured out of this mess."

The Bible clearly speaks about our times and describes them as being perilous. In these last days the church that plans on being the church will face incredible pressure. The *last days* is a biblical term that designates a particular time period with definite events which will take place--that stated time period between the first coming and the second coming of Christ. Let me illustrate this time period with a diagram.

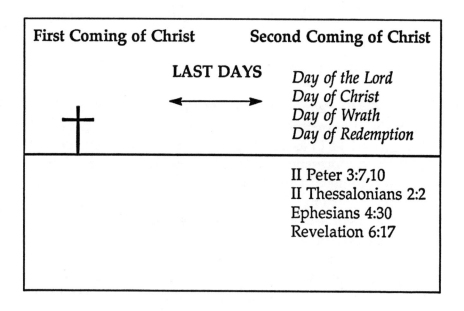

Hebrews 1:1-2. God, after He spoke long ago to the fathers in the prophets in many portions and in many ways, in these *last days* has spoken to us in His Son, whom He appointed heir of all things, through whom also He made the world.

1 Timothy 4:1 Now the Spirit expressly says that in latter times some will depart from the faith, giving heed to deceiving spirits and doctrines of demons,

Micah 4:1. And it will come about in the *last days* that the mountain of the house of the Lord will be established as the chief of the mountains. It will be raised above the hills, and the peoples will stream to it.

Isaiah 2:2. In the *last days*, the mountain of the house of the Lord will be established as the chief of the mountains, and will be raised above the hills; and all nations will stream to it.

Acts 2:17. "And it shall be in the *last days*," God says, "that I will pour forth of My Spirit upon all mankind; and your sons and your daughters shall prophesy, and your young men shall see visions, and your old men shall dream dreams..."

The last days time period will be a time for separation of the two kingdoms--the kingdom of God and the kingdom of Satan. This time period will see the development of two different streams. All people will find themselves in one stream or the other.

	TWO MYSTERIES	
Mystery of	I Timothy 3:15-16	Mystery of
Iniquity	II Thessalonians 2:7	Godliness

	TWO SPIRITS	
Spirit of Error	I John 4:6	Spirit of Truth

	TWO KINGDOMS	
Kingdom of	Colossians 1:13	Kingdom
Darkness	Revelation 16:10	of Light

	TWO WOMEN	
Harlot Woman	Ephesians 5:25-32	Bride
	Revelation 17:5	of Christ

	TWO SEEDS	
The Tares	Matthew 13:24-30	The Wheat

	TWO HOUSES	
The False Church	Matthew 7:24-27	The True
	Hebrews 3:6	Church
	Revelation 17:1-13	

The Apostle Paul wrote to Timothy predicting that this last days period would be perilous. A superficial examination of our current situation both in America and abroad would certainly agree with this prediction. We have diseases such as AIDS, cancer, and other unnamed, uncontrolled plagues which are causing fear in the heart of even the strongest. The epidemic abuse of drugs, political tension and unrest, farm failures, environmental problems, family breakdown, talk of global recession, and the unstable state of both church and government definitely fit the word *perilous*.

In his book, *How Then Shall We Live,* Francis Schaeffer predicted unprecedented pressures. He states, "Overwhelming pressures are being brought to bear on people who have no absolutes, but only have the impoverished values of personal peace and prosperity. The pressures are progressively preparing modern people to accept a manipulative, authoritarian government. Unhappily, many of these pressures are upon us now."

Yet we see a massive increase in knowledge which is not solving these problems. The knowledge increase is causing what is known as *knowledge stress.* Our minds are at the knowledge saturation point. Recent studies have stated that we acquire 2,000 pages of new-found scientific knowledge every twenty-four hours. George Barna in his book *Frog in the Kettle* states that we now have only three percent of the information that will be available to us by the year 2010.

Alvin Toffler in his new book *Power Shift* makes an emphasis on the role knowledge will play in the Twenty-First Century. Toffler explains that the world is experiencing a reconceptualization of power (like a religious conversion) and the wealth creation system. The control of knowledge will be the crux of tomorrow's worldwide struggle for power in every human institution.

Toffler predicts that knowledge will be the new power of the coming century. He predicts that fundamentalism will become a real threat to democracy because of its commitment to theocratic control of the mind and behavior of the individual. Knowledge is the most versatile form of power. With the right kind of knowledge both wealth and force can be multiplied or redirected. Maximum power will come from those who control knowledge. This is an awesome new challenge for the Church as we need to be aware of the struggle for the minds of God's people.

And yet with all our knowledge we have in the southeast parts of America the new rising of the Ku Klux Klan, an ugly past returning to haunt America. In the midst of all this, Christ is building a stable people called His Church--a people who through the wisdom and power of God will rise as the light to conquer the darkness. Yes, these are perilous times, but we have a powerful God who is building a powerful Church which will not be crushed by this sin-sick, pleasure-crazed, lost society. Christ's Church is built for such perilous times!

George Barna, an expert in marketing and research, agrees that these are perilous times. He states, "Unparalleled change will sweep the nation and transform every dimension of life in this country. For the Christian community the 90's will be a time of unprecedented challenge and opportunity. While many of the changes that will occur could threaten the stability and capacity of the church to make an impact on our society, other changes are opening the doors for new forms of ministry."

II Timothy 3:1. But realize this, that in the *last days* difficult times will come.

Let's take a closer look at this word *"perilous"*.

Perilous - to be in danger, high risk, hazardous, difficult, perplexing, particular exposure of person or property to injury, loss or destruction from any dangerous cause, hard to take, hard to bear, troublesome, dangerous, grievous, harsh, fierce savage.

The word *perilous* can be understood by the other

words and phrases commonly associated with it: insecurity, instability, perplexity, uncertainty, cross-fire, vexed, troublesome, in danger, to feel the ground sliding from under one, having the odds against you.

All of these words apply to our times. We all feel the *ground sliding from under us* at times. We are all feeling the squash of a secular society bent on humanism, and now we witness the revival of eastern religions mixed together and presented as the *New Age* philosophy.

Because secular humanism is so prominent we need to delve into it a little more. The Humanist Manifesto written in 1953 and recently edited by Paul Kurtz states what we are up against in these changing times. He states: "We believe, however, that traditional dogmatic or authoritarian religions that place revelation, God, ritual, or creed above human needs and experience do a disservice to the human species. Any account of nature should pass the tests of scientific evidence; in our judgment, the dogmas and myths of traditional religions do not do so. Even at this late date in human history, certain elementary facts based upon the critical use of scientific reason have to be restated. We find insufficient evidence for belief in the existence of a supernatural; it is either meaningless or irrelevant to the question of the survival and fulfillment of the human race. As nontheists, we begin with humans not God, nature not deity. Nature may indeed be broader and deeper than we now know; any new discoveries, however, will but enlarge our knowledge of the natural."

Secular humanism is a religion that dethrones God as the center of life and enshrines man instead. The aim of secular humanism is to replace theism with humanism. It is now recognized by the Supreme Court as a religion called the religious humanists. It is established as part of school curriculum across American and other countries.

The tenets of humanism are atheism, evolution, amorality, autonomous man, and a socialist one world view. Let us quote from the Humanist Manifesto:

> **Atheism:** "We find insufficient evidence for belief in the existence of a supernatural..."

> **Evolution:** "Science affirms that the human species is an emergence from natural evolutionary forces. As far as we know, the total personality is a function of the biological organism transacting in a social environment."

> **Amorality:** "In the area of sexuality we believe that intolerant attitudes are often cultivated by orthodox religions which unduly repress sexual conduct. The right to birth control, abortion, and divorce should be recognized, neither do we wish to prohibit sexual behavior between consenting adults."

> **Autonomous Man:** "Humanism can provide the purpose and inspiration that so many seek. It can give personal meaning and significance to human life. Humans are responsible for what we are or will become. No deity will save us, we must save ourselves."

A comparison of humanism and Christianity allows us to see the clear distinctions:

	CHRISTIANITY	HUMANISM
God	*God is before all things, and in Him all things hold together" (Col 1:17)*	*"We believe that traditional dogmatic, or authoritarian religions that place revelation, God, or ritual or creed above human needs and experiences do a disservice to the human species" (Manifesto II pp.15-16)*
Creation	*God created the heavens and earth. He created man in His own image. (Gen 1:1,26; Heb 11:3)*	*"Science affirms that the human species is an emergence from natural evolutionary forces. As far as we know, the total personality is a function of the biological organism transacting in a social and cultural context" (Manifesto II p.17)*
Salvation	*Salvation comes by repentance and confessing that Jesus Christ is Lord (Acts 2:38; Rom 10:9-10)*	*"Promises of immortal salvation, or fear of eternal damnation are both illusory and harmful. They distract humans from present concerns, from self-actualization, and from rectifying social injustices...There is no credible evidence that life survives the death of the body" (Manifesto II, pp16-17)*

	CHRISTIANITY	HUMANISM
Ethics	The Word of God provides the unchanging foundational rules for ethics.	"We affirm that moral values derive their source from human experiences. Ethics is autonomous and situational, needing no theological or ideological sanction" (Manifesto II p.17)
Family	The family is a basic unit within society where children learn religion, self-government, and education (Eph 6:1-4)	Parent is defined as any person who has primary day-to-day responsibility for any child, and a day care worker can be considered as much a parent as the natural parent...The agency can also step into the family situation to take charge of the child at the request of either the parent or child" (The Separation Illusion, p.132)
Abortion	"Abortion is murder and a crime against God in whose image man was created (Eph 6:1-4)	"The right to birth control, abortion, and divorce should be recognized" Manifesto II, p.18)

10

Twelve Perilous Present Day Conditions

	CHRISTIANITY	HUMANISM
Sexual Perversion	God judges sexual perversions, such as adultery, prostitution, incest, and homosexuality by driving the nation practicing these things out from its land (Lev 18; Rom 1:8,22) Historical examples are Sodom, Rome and Pompeii	"The many varieties of sexual exploration should not in themselves be considered evil. Sexual values and sex acts, like other human values or acts, should be evaluated by whether they frustrate or enhance human fulfillment" (Manifesto II, p.18-19 and A New Bill of Sexual Rights and Responsibilities, p.2)
Socialism	The Bible states that a person will reap (financial reward and sustenance in proportion to the effort put forth (Gal 6:7)	"A socialized and cooperative economic order must be established to the end that the equitable distribution of the means of life be possible. The goal is a free and universal society in which people voluntarily and intelligently cooperate for the common good. Humanists demand a shared life in a shared world." (Humanist Manifesto I)

	CHRISTIANITY	HUMANISM
Nationalism	God values individual nations just as He does individual people. He has specific purposes for the nations just as He does for people (Christian History of the Constitution, pp.3-4; Teaching and Learning America's Christian History, pp. 142-152)	"We deplore the divisions of human kind on nationalistic grounds. We have reached a turning point in human history where the best option is to transcend the limits of national sovereignty and move toward the building of a world community in which all sectors of the human family can participate. Thus we look forward to the development of a system of world law and a world order based upon transnational federal government" (Manifesto II, p.21)
Education	The Bible clearly requires the parents to bring up their children and educate them in the ways of God. Isaiah 54:16 states, "All your children shall be taught of the Lord and great shall be the peace and prosperity of your children."	Education is self-realization and self-development because the truth is within each person and must be allowed to be expressed. Education is freedom from restraints and freedom from any idea of truth originating outside himself.

These are times of great change and challenge for those who will take a stand against such deception as humanism. This deceptive philosophy has crept into education, politics, law, media, religion, and medicine. True Christians must take time to identify any satanic infiltration that has taken place personally, domestically, and politically. These insidious philosophies are working on the minds, values, concepts, and convictions of the people of God. Let us arise and take a stand! Revival occurs when Christians influence the world. Apostasy take place when the world influences Christians.

> *Colossians 2:8.* "See to it that no one takes you captive through philosophy and empty deception, according to the tradition of men, according to the elementary principles of the world, rather than according to Christ."

> *II Thessalonians 2:10-11.* "...and with all the deception of wickedness for those who perish, because they did not receive the love of the truth so as to be saved. And for this reason God will send upon them a deluding influence so that they might believe what is false."

God has promised to raise up a standard when the enemy comes in like a flood. You are a vital part of that standard when you allow the Word and power of Christ to work in and through your life. *Now* is the time for every man, woman and child to dedicate themselves to the reliability of God's Word, and the true unshakable values of God's Kingdom.

These are *perilous times!* We must rise to our feet as the true people of God who have a hope and a destiny in our God and His Word through the Holy Spirit.

> *Jeremiah 29:11-13.* "For I know the plans that I have for you," declares the Lord, "plans for welfare and not for calamity to give you a future and a hope.

> Then you will call upon Me and come and pray to
> Me, and I will listen to you. And you will seek Me
> and find Me, when you search for Me with all your
> heart."

In the midst of changing values, changing standards, situational ethics, and relativism, there will be a people anchored to the Rock. The Church will not be defeated or devoured by the enemies of our day. Perilous times can only purge us of our dross, our lukewarmness, and our religious spirit as we stand our ground and be Christ's Church in perilous times! Christ's Church will not be threatened by the gates of hell!

> *Matthew 16:16-18.* And Simon Peter answered and
> said, "Thou art the Christ, the Son of the living God."
> And Jesus answered and said to him, "Blessed are
> you, Simon Barjona, because flesh and blood did not
> reveal this to you, but My Father who is in heaven.
> And I also say to you that you are Peter, and upon
> this rock I will build My church: and the gates of
> Hades shall not overpower it."

There are at least twelve perilous conditions the Church either will face or is facing in these last days. Before we list the twelve, let us quote our text and various translations of this Scripture:

II Timothy 3:1.

(NIV)	But mark this: There will be *terrible times* in the last days.
(NAS)	But realize this, that in the last days *difficult times* will come.
(TLB)	You may as well know this too, that in the last days it is going to be *very difficult* to be a Christian
(RSV)	But understand this, that in the last days there will come *times of stress.*
(CL)	Now this know, that in the last days *perilous periods*

14

will be present.

(AMP) But understand this, that in the last days there will set in *perilous times of great stress and trouble* hard to deal with and hard to bear.

The perilous conditions we face are described as terrible times, difficult times, times of stress and trouble. The Church will not only face twelve perilous conditions, but will be triumphant in the midst of them!

1. The Perilous Condition of Deception.

Matthew 24:4-5,11,24. And Jesus answered and said to them, "See to it that no one misleads you. For many will come in My name, saying 'I am the Christ,' and will mislead many. And many false prophets will arise and will mislead many. For false Christs and false prophets will arise and will show great signs and wonders, so as to mislead, if possible, even the elect."

Deception is rampant with the rise of new age, secular humanism, eastern religions, unbiblical Christianity and the occult.

2. The Perilous Condition of Fear.

Matthew 24:6. "And you will be hearing of wars and rumors of wars; see that you are not frightened, for those things must take place, but that is not yet the end."

Luke 21:26. "Men fainting from fear and the expectation of the things which are coming upon the world; for the powers of the heavens will be shaken."

People fear war, environmental decay, uncontrolled

15

violence, inner city destruction, AIDS, cancer, and other incurable diseases.

3. The Perilous Condition of Persecution.

> *Matthew 24:9.* "Then they will deliver you up to tribulation, and will kill you, and you will be hated by all nations on account of My name."

Twentieth Century persecution of the church in all parts of the world has claimed thousands of lives and removed some great leaders. Persecution may come in a violent form or a non-violent form. The United States is experiencing a non-violent persecution through the media and modern day mind-set against everything for which the church stands.

4. The Perilous Condition of Unresolved Offenses.

> *Matthew 24:10.* "And at that time many will fall away and will betray one another and hate one another."

5. The Perilous Condition of False Ministries.

> *Matthew 24:11.* "And many false prophets will arise, and will mislead many.

> *Jeremiah 23:14.* "Also among the prophets of Jerusalem I have seen a horrible thing: the committing of adultery and walking in falsehood; and they strengthen the hands of evildoers, so that no one has turned back from his wickedness. All of them have become to Me like Sodom, and her inhabitants like Gomorrah."

> *Isaiah 3:12.* O My people! Their oppressors are

16

children, and women rule over them. O My people!
Those who guide you lead you astray, and confuse
the direction of your paths.

6. *The Perilous Condition of Loss of Spiritual Passion.*

Matthew 24:12-14. And because lawlessness is
increased, most people's love will grow cold. But
the one who endures to the end, it is he who shall be
saved. And this gospel of the kingdom shall be
preached in the whole world for a witness to all the
nations, and then the end shall come.

Hebrews 10:38-39. But My righteous one shall live
by faith; and if he shrinks back, My soul has no
pleasure in Him. But we are not of those who
shrink back to destruction, but of those who have
faith to the preserving of the soul.

7. *The Perilous Condition of Apostasy.*

I Timothy 4:1. But the Spirit explicitly says that in
later times some will fall away from the faith, paying
attention to deceitful spirits and doctrines of demons.

8. *The Perilous Condition of Demonic Spirits.*

I Timothy 4:1-2. But the Spirit explicitly says that in
later times some will fall away from the faith, paying
attention to deceitful spirits and doctrines of demons,
by means of the hypocrisy of liars seared in their
own conscience as with a branding iron...

James 4:7. Submit therefore to God. Resist the devil
and he will flee from you.

9. *The Perilous Condition of a Seared Conscience.*

I Timothy 4:2. By means of the hypocrisy of liars seared in their own conscience as with a branding iron...

10. *The Perilous Condition of Human Depravity.*

II Timothy 3:1-8. But realize this, that in the last days difficult times will come. For men will be lovers of self, lovers of money, boastful, arrogant, revilers, disobedient to parents, ungrateful, unholy, unloving, irreconcilable, malicious gossips, without self-control, brutal, haters of good, treacherous, reckless, conceited, lovers of pleasure rather than lovers of God; holding to a form of godliness, although they have denied its power; and avoid such men as these. For among them are those who enter into households and captivate weak women weighed down with sins, led on by various impulses, always learning and never able to come to the knowledge of the truth. And just as Jannes and Jambres opposed Moses, so these men also oppose the truth, men of depraved mind, rejected as regards the faith.

11. *The Perilous Condition of Scoffers.*

II Peter 3:3. Know this first of all, that in the last days mockers will come with their mocking, following after their own lusts.

12. *The Perilous Condition of the Antichrist.*

I John 2:18,22. Children, it is the last hour; and just as you hear that antichrist is coming, even now many antichrists have arisen; from this we know that it is the last hour. Who is the liar but the one who denies that Jesus is the Christ? This is the antichrist, the one who denies the Father and the Son.

I John 4:3. And every spirit that does not confess Jesus is not from God; and this is the spirit of the antichrist, of which you have heard that it is coming, and now it is already in the world.

II John 1:7. For many deceivers have gone out into the world, those who do not acknowledge Jesus Christ as coming in the flesh. This is the deceiver and the antichrist.

The only way the Church can successfully face these perilous conditions is to become well equipped for spiritual battles. This calls for well equipped, wise leaders who know how to prepare God's people to stand against deception, fear, pressures, false ministry, etc. We must hear God's wake-up call. These could be great days of revival and influence for God's people or terrible days of defeat and disillusionment. Our response to God's call to prepare ourselves may be the deciding factor.

Isaiah 51:9,15-17. Awake, awake, put on strength, o arm of the Lord; awake as in the days of old, the generations of long ago. Was it not Thou who cut Rahab in pieces, who pierced the dragon? "For I am the Lord your God, who stirs up the sea and its waves roar (the Lord of hosts is his name). And I have put My words in your mouth, and have covered you with the shadow of My hand, to establish the heavens, to found the earth, and to say to Zion, 'You are My people.'" Rouse yourself! Rouse yourself! Arise, O Jerusalem, you who have drunk from the Lord's hand the cup of His anger; the chalice of reeling you have drained to the dregs.

2

Understanding Our Spiritual Roots

"As we prepare for this final battle as Christ's Church, it's crucial to understand where we have been."

To understand the direction in which the Church is going today, we must understand her past. We must grasp how the Church began, what she is, and where she has traveled up to now.

Above all, we must remind ourselves that the Church is Christ's Church, created for His purposes. She is His concept, and Christ is the Head of the Church. When Peter declared Christ's identity (Matthew 16:16-18), Jesus revealed the purpose in His first coming: to lay the cornerstone of the Church. When Jesus told His disciples the way in which they were to go out and preach the Kingdom (Matthew 18:16-19), He also declared that the Church was given power over the enemy and power to discipline her own. Though Christ spoke of both apostasy and heresy in the Church, He never spoke of His Church failing. He never spoke of abandoning His Church for something better. Christ is committed to building His Church and finishing His work.

BIRTH OF THE CHURCH

What kind of Church did Christ plan to build? What Christ promised in the Gospels concerning His Church we see partly fulfilled in the Book of Acts.

As we study Acts, the connection between Old Testament prophets and New Testament apostles becomes obvious. The first apostles had no New Testament, but relied upon the Old Testament law and prophets. As God moved in miraculous and wonderful ways, the apostles depended heavily upon the Old Testament for guidance and confirmation, especially on the Old Testament prophets.

In Acts 2 we see the day of Pentecost with the outpouring of the Holy Spirit. On this occasion, it is the apostle Peter who rises in the midst of the brethren and offers scriptural explanation for the event. The apostle Peter reaches back to the Old Testament prophet Joel, and together they lay an apostolic foundation for the Church.

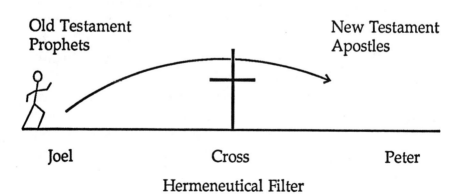

Old Testament
Prophets

New Testament
Apostles

Joel   Cross   Peter

Hermeneutical Filter

Joel the prophet
Joel 2:28-29

"And it will come about after this that I will pour out My Spirit on all mankind; and your sons and daughters will prophesy, your old men will dream dreams, your young men will see visions. And even on the male and female servants I will pour out My Spirit in those days."

Peter the apostle
Acts 2:16-17

"But this is what was spoken of through the prophet Joel: 'And it shall be in the last days,' God says, 'That I will pour forth of My spirit upon all mankind; and your sons and your daughters shall prophesy, and your young men shall see visions, and your old men shall dream dreams...'"

THE LAST DAYS

Although Acts 2:16-17 is significant for several reasons, we will focus here on Peter's reference to the "last days," for it provides the frame of reference more so today. The apostle defined for us the time period in which we live today, and it began on the day of Pentecost.

"It shall come to pass in the last days," prophesied Joel. Peter, in apostolic authority, declared the proper interpretation of this scripture: that the last days had begun to come to pass in his own time. That was the beginning of the last days. For the sake of clarity, let us define the *last days* as that time period between the *first* coming and the *second* coming of the Lord Jesus Christ.

We have already laid some groundwork for understanding the last days in the first chapter of this book. Let us place another stone on the foundation we have laid.

Other scriptures which refer to the last days:

Isaiah 2:1-4. The word which Isaiah the son of Amoz saw concerning Judah and Jerusalem. Now it will come about that in the last days, the mountain of the house of the Lord will be established as the chief of the mountains, and will be raised above the hills; and all the nations will stream to it. And many peoples will come and say, "Come, let us go up to the mountain of the Lord, to the house of the God of Jacob; that He may teach us concerning His ways, and that we may walk in His paths." For the law will go forth from Zion, and the word of the Lord from Jerusalem. And He will judge between the nations, and will render decisions for many peoples; and they will hammer their swords into plowshares, and their spears into pruning hooks. Nation will not lift up sword against nation, and never again will they learn war.

Micah 4:1,2. And it will come about in the last days that the mountain of the house of the Lord will be established as the chief of the mountains. It will be raised above the hills, and the peoples will stream to it. And many nations will come and say, "Come and let us go up to the mountain of the Lord and to the house of the God of Jacob, that He may teach us about His ways and that we may walk in His paths." For from Zion will go forth the law, even the word of the Lord from Jerusalem.

I Timothy 4:1. But the Spirit explicitly says that in later times some will fall away from the faith, paying attention to deceitful spirits and doctrines of demons.

King Nebuchadnezzar's Dream.

Another way of seeing the last days time period

24

clearly is shown in Daniel's interpretation of King Nebuchadnezzar's dream about the image of the man (Daniel 2:31-45). By superimposing the image of the man upon our diagram, we can see the last days time period coinciding with the image's legs and feet. Historically, the prophecy of Daniel has been fulfilled down to the feet of the image, which we are now approaching.

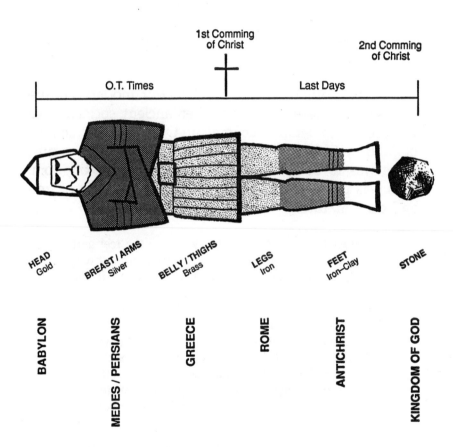

Note: The stone strikes the feet of the image in a final blow to destroy the kingdoms of this world. The stone represents the Kingdom of God, or the *stone people*--the living stones who make up the church of Jesus Christ in these Last Days.

The fourth kingdom, which was made of iron and was the legs of the image, predicted the rule of the Roman Empire.

> *Daniel 2:40.* There will be a fourth kingdom as strong as iron; inasmuch as iron crushes and shatters all things, so, like iron that breaks in pieces, it will crush and break all these in pieces.

The Roman Empire parallels our modern culture and society more than any other ancient society. (To explore this in detail, I recommend Dr. Francis Schaeffer's book, *How Should We Then Live?*) After the Roman rule, there was to be one more world-dominating kingdom. This was pictured in the feet of the image made of iron and clay mixture.

> *Daniel 2:41-43.* And in that you saw the feet and toes, partly of potter's clay and partly of iron, it will be a divided kingdom; but it will have in it the toughness of iron, inasmuch as you saw the iron mixed with common clay. And as the toes of the feet were partly of iron and partly of pottery, so some of the kingdom will be strong and part of it will be brittle. And in that you saw the iron mixed with common clay, they will combine with one another in the seed of men; but they will not adhere to one another, even as iron does not combine with pottery.

This is the last kingdom to come to power before Christ's kingdom establishes full dominion over the earth for ever and ever.

Daniel 2:44-45. And in the days of those kings the God of heaven will set up a kingdom which will never be destroyed, and that kingdom will not be left for another people; it will crush and put an end to all these kingdoms, but it will itself endure forever.

The stone kingdom cut out of the mountain without hands will crush all rule and authority that has passed from kingdom to kingdom through the ages. The Church today constitutes the people of the stone kingdom, and we will face the last great battle against the kingdom of antichrist, as prophesied in the Book of Revelation. This kingdom of antichrist will have its roots in spiritual Babylon and will be judged by Christ and His overcoming Church.

Revelation 17:1-6. And one of the seven angels who had the seven bowls came and spoke with me, saying, "Come here, I shall show you the judgment of the great harlot who sits on many waters, with whom the kings of the earth committed acts of immorality, and those who dwell on the earth were made drunk with the wine of her immorality." And he carried me away in the Spirit into a wilderness; and I saw a woman sitting on a scarlet beast, full of blasphemous names, having seven heads and ten horns. And the woman was clothed in purple and scarlet, and adorned with gold and precious stones and pearls, having in her hand a gold cup full of abominations and of the unclean things of her immorality, and upon her forehead a name was written, a mystery, "Babylon the great, the mother of harlots and of the abominations of the earth." And I saw the woman drunk with the blood of the saints, and with the blood of the witnesses of Jesus. And when I saw her, I wondered greatly.

As Jeremiah stood before Judah prior to her overthrow by Babylon, so the Church faces its own spiritual Babylon. We are seeing the fulfillment of Daniel's prophecy and John's prophecy in Revelation 17:1-10. Our frame of reference is that we are in the latter end of the time period called the last days. We now look to the consummation of all things, when the Church will triumph and be exalted to the mountain peaks. As we prepare for this final battle as Christ's Church, it's crucial to understand where we have been and where we are going. The following historical overview will help us understand the spiritual condition of the Church today.

CHURCH HISTORY

The New Testament describes the earthly ministry of Christ and the early years of the Church. The Gospels establish Christ's three-and-a-half years of ministry, His death, His resurrection, His ascension, His promised return. Upon that foundation stands the Church. We also know the Church began on the day of Pentecost in A.D. 33, and that the Holy Spirit first came in power then. Because we believe the Book of Acts presents a picture of the Church as she should be, we should use Acts as a guide for Church doctrine and practice more than what we see happening in the Church today (or any other day, for that matter). Acts is an historical account of the first one hundred years of the Church. Because it is historical some expositors say we cannot use it to establish doctrine. To this I say we need both Acts and the epistles to establish doctrine, for Acts gives us an inside look at the Church Christ said He would build.

Before the Decline

Christ predicted that the gates of hell could not

prevail against His Church (Matthew 16:18), and that is the kind of Church we see in Acts. It was a powerful group, one that turned Jerusalem, a major city, upside down.

We find the Church filled with the Holy Spirit, led by the apostles and prophets, and casting demons out of people. We find the Church also rebuking people. For what—for not giving money? No, but for lying to the Holy Spirit, as did Ananias and Sapphira (Acts 5:1-10). The early Church moved in the power and conviction of the Holy Spirit.

A capsule study of the Church in the Book of Acts, before the historical decline that began around A.D. 100, shows a divine organization with a truly divine and miraculous personality. Some of the traits and accomplishments of the early Church:

1. Unity (Acts 1:14, 2:1).
2. Powerful in prayer (1:14).
3. Founded on the Word of God (1:15-20 and 2:16,29,30 and 3:22-25 and 4:23-30).
4. Led by the Spirit (11:12-14).
5. Recognized and submitted to the Headship of Christ (2:36-38).
6. Ministered to the whole person (6:1-6).
7. Produced disciples (2:42 and 6:7; Matthew 28:19).
8. Produced ministries (13:1-3 and 16:1-5; Philippians 2:19-22; II Timothy 1:9,10).
9. Planted other local churches (14:21-23 and 16:5 and 20:12-30).
10. Responded correctly to trials and persecutions (4:1-31 and 5:17-42).
11. Experienced the miraculous (3:1-10 and 8:39,40).
12. Produced apostolic ministry (13:1-5).
13. Received angelic ministry (12:7-10).

14. Exercised authority over the powers of hell (8:7,8).
15. Caused city-wide revivals (Acts 8:8).
16. Fulfilled in part the Great Commission (Acts 1:8).
17. Ministered to the nations (16:1-5 and 18:23 and 19:21,22 and 20:5-12).
18. Preached the Kingdom of God (8:12 and 14:22 and 19:8 and 20:25 and 28:23,31).
19. Dealt with the occult (8:9-13 and 13:6-12).
20. Strong and pure character (11:26).
21. Had many important truths:
    • Apostolic doctrine (Acts 2:42; Hebrews 6:1-6);
    • Salvation by faith (Acts 16:30,31);
    • Water baptism by immersion (Acts 8:38,39);
    • Holiness (II Corinthians 6:17);
    • Healing (Acts 5:16);
    • Baptism of the Holy Spirit (Acts 2:1-6);
    • Laying on of hands (Acts 13:3);
    • Resurrection of the dead (Acts 9:36-43);
    • Praise and joy in abundance (Acts 13:52 and 16:25).
22. Had all of these ministries functioning:
    • Twelve apostles (1:12-26);
    • Seven deacons (6:1-7);
    • Evangelists (8:6,13,40);
    • Prophets (11:27-30);
    • Elders (15:2-5);
    • Pastors/Teachers (13:1-6);
    • Apostles (15:1-4).
23. Flowed in the nine gifts of the Holy Spirit (I Corinthians 12:7-11)

Decline Foreknown
    From the very beginning of Christianity the Church was in danger of altering its God-given intentions because of satanic and cultural pressures. Tendencies emerged to change the doctrines of Christ and separate Christians

into argumentative groups. Some wanted to mix the ideas and practices of Judaism with Christianity. Others tended to import pagan philosophies and customs. Still others simply misunderstood some aspects of Christianity. During the lifetime of the first apostles such tendencies were held in check. The New Testament letters show how the apostles held Christianity to its original character. But after the apostles passed off the scene, movements toward deviation progressed more rapidly.

One generation would make alterations in doctrine and practice and the next generation would accept changes without question and add some of their own. Over a period of several generations the changes became extreme. Elements of paganism sifted in and the Church began its slow decline into the dark ages.

Both society and culture at times try to adopt the Church as one of its own institutions, thus neutralizing its impact or binding its influence toward social ends. Culture often tries to develop a "folk religion" version of the Church out of failure to understand biblical Christianity. This process dampens purposefulness and militancy in congregations, encumbers Christianity with unproductive traditions, and undermines vigorous pursuit of Christ's commission.

The spiritual and moral decline of the Church was foretold in Scripture. In the New Testament Scripture, it is found in Matthew 24:10, II Thessalonians 2:10, and I Timothy 4:1. The state of the Church in decline is described in some Old Testament Scriptures such as Joel 1:1-25 and Jeremiah 2:13-15.

Matthew 24:10. And at that time many will fall away and will betray one another and hate one another.

II Thessalonians 2:10. And with all the deception of

31

wickedness for those who perish, because they did not receive the love of the truth so as to be saved.

Joel 1:4,7,9,15. What the gnawing locust has left, the swarming locust has eaten; and what the swarming locust has left, the creeping locust has eaten; and what the creeping locust has left, the stripping locust has eaten...It has made my vine a waste, and my fig tree splinters. It has stripped them bare and cast them away; their branches have become white....The grain offering and the libation are cut off from the house of the Lord. The priests mourn, the ministers of the Lord....Alas for the day! For the day of the Lord is near, and it will come as destruction from the Almighty.

Jeremiah 2:13-15. For my people have committed two evils: they have forsaken Me, the fountain of living waters, to hew for themselves cisterns, broken cisterns, that can hold no water. Is Israel a slave? Or is he a homeborn servant? Why has he become a prey? The young lions have roared at him, they have roared loudly. And they have made his land a waste; his cities have been destroyed, without inhabitant.

The decline of the Church was also foreshadowed symbolically in Scripture. Here are three events that could speak to us on how the Church would decline: the fall of Adam and Eve (Genesis 3:1-23), the fall of Samson (Judges 16:19-23), and the captivity of Israel (Lamentations).

In the fall of Samson, as shown on the next page, we have an analogous description of the Church in decline.

32

Samson	Church
• Seven locks of hair cut	• Seven doctrines lost
• Affliction, weakness	• Under persecution
• No presence of God	• Spiritual hardness
• Eyes removed	• Spiritual blindness
• Brought down	• Spiritual decline
• Bound to prison house grinding wheel	• Spiritual bondage to ritualism
• Mocked and ridiculed	• Mocked for corruption

In Judah's captivity as described in the Book of Lamentations, we also have a detailed analogy for the decline of the Church.

Lamentations 1:1-3,8; 2:14; 5:1-3. How lonely sits the city that was full of people! She has become like a widow who was once great among the nations! She who was a princess among the provinces has become a forced laborer! She weeps bitterly in the night, and her tears are on her cheeks; she has none to comfort her among all her lovers. All her friends have dealt treacherously with her; they have become her enemies. Judah has gone into exile under affliction, and under harsh servitude...Her adversaries have become her masters, her enemies prosper, for the Lord has caused her grief because of the multitude of her transgressions...Jerusalem sinned greatly, therefore she has become an unclean thing. All who honored her despise her because they have seen her nakedness; even she herself groans and turns away...Your prophets have seen for you false and foolish visions; and they have not exposed your iniquity so as to restore you from captivity but they have seen for you false and misleading oracles...Remember, O Lord, what has befallen us; look, and see our reproach! Our inheritance has been turned over to strangers, our houses to aliens. We have become orphans without a father, our mothers are like widows.

Causes of the Decline

The causes of the Church's decline are many. The following list focuses on the sins that also threaten the Church of the 20th century.

1. Loss of faith.
2. Belief in a lie.
3. Compromise of the truth.
4. Loss of vision.
5. Loss of character (II Peter 1:3-11).
6. Spiritual blindness.
7. Lack of a single heart/single eye toward God (Revelation 3:18; Genesis 3:1-7).
8. Forfeiture of truth to follow favorite lusts (Ephesians 2:3; II Peter 3:3).
9. Departure from their first love (I John 4:18; Revelation 2:4).
10. Tolerance of false teachers going uncorrected (Acts 2:28-30; II Peter 2:1; Revelation 2:14,15).
11. Tolerance of false prophets going uncorrected (II Peter 2:3, 13-19; Revelation 2:20-23).
12. Lukewarmness (Revelation 3:15,16).
13. Worldliness (I John 2:15-17; Revelation 3:17).
14. Self-sufficiency.
15. Contempt for spiritual government (II John 9,10).
16. Corrupted leadership that sought position above service.

Historical Decline of the Church

The biblical record of Church history, including the Book of Acts and the epistles, ends around 100 A.D. After this we must look to other records from the early Church. The list below provides a condensed record of major events illustrating the decline of the Church in its first three centuries.

A.D.

100 Last of twelve apostles dies
110 Last of Church fathers dies
130 Laying on of hands declines
140 Confusion over the office of prophecy
150 Gifts of the Spirit become narrow in practice
160 Plurality of eldership concept declines, local church government changes
180 Local church autonomy increasingly given to bishops
187 First infant baptism
205 Priesthood of all believers reduced in practice
210 Official Church leaders assume title of *priests*
220 Heresies unchecked by Church creedal statements
240 Double standards of holiness for ministers' laity
250 Clergy established as elective office
300 Justification by faith alone challenged

During the reign of Constantine I, the Church was removed from outlaw status and Christianity became the official state religion. Every citizen had to become a member of the Church--or be killed. The Church became a state church, with emperor Constantine as its titular head, the worst thing that ever happened to the Church. Unsaved people were baptized and attended church only for fear of their lives. Naturally, corruption set into the

Church. Every sign of spiritual health declined--worship, eldership, laying on of hands, prophecies, the apostleship and the office of prophet. Church unity fragmented as ecclesiastical orders and organizations vied for power with doctrines and separate headquarters. The Church lost the Spirit of what God was doing.

Church history continued its decline into the Dark Ages, which we generally place from 500 to 1200 A.D. It was an age of priestly immorality, and heretical doctrines. Priestly celibacy, never required by the Bible, became a source of temptation, sin and disillusionment for the Church.

The Church reached her darkest hour around the end of the Dark Ages. Mass was given in Latin, a language not known by the common people. Imagine going to church and hearing everything in Spanish or Russian. You would leave a service with only a set of images and feelings, with your faith totally uninformed and undirected. But it was worse than that--the Bible was also in a *foreign* language (Latin) as well, and only the scholars approved by a corrupted Church could promulgate doctrine. The common people could not own a Bible--in fact, some were burned at the stake for having one!

Reformation

Access to the Word of God became one of the rallying cries of a movement that gradually resulted in the religious reformation of the Church in Europe. It began with translations into the common languages, and was accelerated with mass printing of the Bible on the newly invented printing press. Men like Gutenberg and Zinzendorf led the movement to put the Bible in the hands of the common people. Many were persecuted and even killed for their efforts.

As the common people began to read the Bible, they began to ask hard questions of a Church which they already understood to be corrupt: "Is purgatory spiritual? Why do we have priestly celibacy? Will crawling up steps on broken glass really profit my soul?" The movement which would become the Reformation began to rise in the 1300's and more fully blossomed under Martin Luther in the early 1500s.

An Augustinian monk and professor of biblical exegesis, Luther did a verse-by-verse exposition of the Book of Romans. He came to the understanding that no man could receive salvation through a priest, bishop, or pope, but only through Christ Himself. The beginning of the Reformation itself is usually set as Oct. 31, 1517. On this day, Luther nailed his "Ninety-Five Theses" on the door of the Palace Church in Wittenberg, in protest against the sale of Church indulgences for sin. Luther was hunted and feared for his life, but was hidden and protected for years by powerful friends.

Luther preached and wrote that "the just shall live by faith, not by works;" that salvation came through repentance and faith in the blood of Christ, not through the sacraments or clergy of the Catholic Church. Personal faith, meaningful personal relationship with Christ, was restored.

The Anabaptist movement appeared later in the Reformation, and was a subject of controversy even among reformers. The meaning of their name (*Ana* means *re*) explains their movement. They re-baptized many adult Christians, with full immersion instead of sprinkling. They became known as *dunkers*, and aroused heated disputes with Lutherans, who still sprinkled. Lutherans sometimes went so far as drowning Anabaptists, a tragic event in what was a great spiritual movement. Nonetheless, the Anabaptists restored the truth of water baptism of adults to the Church.

Another important event in the spiritual life of the Church, not long after the Reformation, was the ministry of John Wesley. He was one of the most educated and enlightened men in Europe. John and his brother Charles founded the Methodist movement with their first church in 1738. John was a magnificent preacher, whose central message was holiness and personal accountability to God. Charles wrote many of the great hymns that we still sing today. Together they started a major revival movement.

So we see the decline of the Church, which was foretold in prophecy, experienced in history, and somewhat reversed in a great Reformation. We still hear echoes of these events in the doctrines, structure and personality of the major church denominations today. Justification by faith, believers' baptism, and holiness are all an important part of the faith of most Christians today. For a more detailed description of the Church's spiritual condition today, we will turn to a study of major spiritual movements of the 20th Century.

3

Understanding Major Spiritual Movements

"When the Holy Spirit moves upon the Church, it must usually bring the Church back from a backslidden spiritual condition."

The Holy Spirit sends seasons of refreshing upon Christ's Church. Peter declared to his generation:

> *Acts 3:19.* Repent therefore and return, that your sins may be wiped away, in order that times of refreshing may come from the presence of the Lord.

God determines these seasons, and governs their coming and going. We cannot stop them or start them, we can only respond to them. That does not, however, excuse us from our responsibility to fast, pray and ask God for a fresh move of His Holy Spirit. But we should be instructed to try to discern the times and seasons of the Lord, to know His day of visitation. Jesus said to the

Jews in Jerusalem:

> *Luke 19:42,44.* If you had known in this day, even you, the things which make for peace! But now they have been hidden from your eyes...because you did not recognize the time of your visitation.

In every visitation there are those like the men of Issachar, "who understood the times with knowledge of what Israel should do" (I Chronicles 12:32). God determined to pour out His Spirit on the day of Pentecost; that was a special day on His calendar. Those who responded were those who followed the Lord and obeyed His teachings. They were in prayer for a period of ten days.

It seems that all visitations are prefaced by prayer. Prayer prepares the soil of people's hearts to respond to God's outpouring of His Spirit. These outpourings may be called spiritual movements. Most movements generate organizations, denominations, universities or seminaries which often bear the name of a key person or emphasized doctrine of the movement. These institutions grow out of spiritual movements as man struggles to define or perhaps even control what has happened. As spiritual movements are organized, some of the spontaneous spiritual power and life that began the movement is lost. Our interest in this book is not primarily the institutions that follow a movement of the Holy Spirit, but the movement itself.

When the Holy Spirit moves upon the Church, it must usually bring the Church back from a backslidden spiritual condition. As the Church responds with repentance, prayer, cleansing and a return to biblical order, the blessings of God return, along with the power and presence of the Holy Spirit. There have been many movings of the Holy Spirit in many different countries of the world. Some are only known by those who experienced the season of revival in that country. Other movements are known because they affected many nations at the same time. Let's discuss three significant movements which have affected the world since the turn of the Twentieth Century. These movements were not always received as "from God". In fact controversy and division characterized all three movements. Nevertheless they had spiritual impact.

Three significant spiritual movements which have affected the world since the turn of the 20th century are: the Azusa Street revival (1906), the Latter Rain revival (1948), and the Charismatic Renewal (1968).

MAJOR 20th CENTURY MOVEMENTS

Azusa Street Revival

At the turn of the 20th century, the movement that eventually took form as the Assemblies of God and Pentecostal denominations began in a little church in Los Angeles. The Christians there began to pray in this little church, both white and black folks, and the Holy Spirit fell in a way which had not been seen for hundreds of years. People were baptized in the Holy Spirit and gave evidence by speaking in other tongues. As the movement grew, it held the personality of that first gathering: very emotional in worship and in the use of the gifts of the Holy Spirit.

Many books have documented this as one of the greatest revivals in history. Nonetheless, at the time, many other Christians labeled it as *heresy* because of its emotional intensity. Unfortunately some of the valid experiences were later taken to extremes as human feelings and fleshly egos of man were lifted up in sin and pride.

Out of this movement sprang up many different Pentecostal groups that later divided over doctrine and church structure. As these sub-movements divided and organized themselves, the seeds of denominations were further sown. The Assemblies of God, Foursquare, Pentecostal Church of God and many other denominations were born.

One major problem, common with many movements, was that what began spontaneously by the Spirit was eventually manipulated and marketed by man. Some powerful evangelists and preachers were found living a double life. Alcohol, abusive sexual habits and unethical finances began to surface and caused great disillusionment among the churches. Although the false ministries were revealed, there were may true ministries which kept their integrity and moved on in the Spirit.

It was no coincidence that the era of the deliverance and healing evangelist came soon after the 1906 Azusa Street revival. The peak of these ministries came between 1930 and 1950. Some of these people were William Branham, Gordon Lindsay, T.L. Osborne, Oral Roberts, Kathryn Kuhlman, Kenneth Hagin and many more. Many of these tent evangelists drew crowds of 15,000 to 20,000 per meeting! Eventually some converted their tent ministries into institutions with buildings, and then launched television ministries. Unfortunately, some ministries with questionable methods and character were also mixed with true, godly ministries. Nonetheless, the truths deposited in the Church during these years still live on, as truth always does.

Latter Rain Revival

This revival followed the Azusa Street revival by about forty years. Once again, the Church had fallen prey to carnal manipulation, shallow preaching, low moral standards, dead ritualism, and division. God initiated this much-needed time and season of visitation. The Latter Rain revival began practicing the doctrine of laying on of hands for purposes beyond deliverance and healing. This came as a *new revelation* at the time. The ministry of the presbytery was birthed during this outpouring of the Spirit, and the laying on of hands by presbyters with prophecy was the truth revealed.

It was a year of important events: in 1948, the Jews became a nation in the state of Israel, and the Latter Rain movement began. The Latter Rain movement emphasized the act of true biblical worship with singing of praise, as a unit of people, and not just shouting, "Praise the Lord!" individually, as did the Pentecostals. The idea of worship and praise with instruments became a beautiful truth in experience. It is now practiced by thousands of churches, many of them in mainline denominations such as Presbyterian, Methodist and Baptist.

In the Latter Rain, the Holy Spirit moved on groups of worshippers, with melodious praise flowing up and down like rhythmic waves of gentle tropical breezes, and then rising to a crescendo of loud praise with much enthusiasm. While many churches accepted this movement, many also resisted it, including some Pentecostal brethren. Some elements of the Latter Rain revival began to go the way of all flesh. Prophecy was abused. Churches were split over it, and some extreme perfectionism teachings were popular at the same time. Immorality and misuse of finances were also surfacing. Yet in spite of its failings, this movement gave to the Body of Christ some teachings that were great spiritual deposits from the Holy Spirit. *From this we must learn not to reject a truth just because it is mishandled or associated with problematic personalities.*

Charismatic Renewal

The Charismatic renewal took place about 20 years after the 1948 Latter Rain revival. Churches that experienced the Latter Rain revival had failed to make any real influence on the broader Body of Christ. Truths of the revival were mainly preserved within their own ranks. Partly due to this failure to reach the broader Body of Christ, the Church at large was failing in its mission to reach its generation. But God moved once again, though in a fashion totally different from the earlier two revivals of this century.

In 1967-68, America was in the throes of welcoming the *Baby Boom* generation to the responsibilities of adult life, but the *boomers* were not buying it. Every legitimate value was questioned. Riots on college campuses shook the nation, with the most terrible example being the Kent State riot that left four students dead. While the Church appeared stagnant, every vice was thriving: drugs, questionable rock-n-roll music, sexual permissiveness, and violence. But God did not leave this generation untouched.

God moved upon an entire nation of rebellious young *longhairs* in a spiritual movement that became known as the Jesus People movement. Thousands were swept into the Kingdom of Heaven--but not into the traditional churches. Why?

The Church was unprepared for such a surprising harvest of unusual people. New churches sprang up almost overnight to accommodate the harvest. Dead churches began to open to the Holy Spirit, resulting in a mass renewal among denominations from Catholics to the Presbyterians. New believers desperately needed teaching on the Holy Spirit, the gifts of the Spirit, walking in the Spirit, the New Testament Church, worship and other foundations of Christian living.

God raised up a number of charismatic teachers that held massive teaching conferences attended by Pentecostal, denominational, independent, and *Jesus People* Christians. Churches that embraced the Charismatic renewal grew supernaturally. Large churches, no longer unusual, became the norm. Yet many of these quick growing large churches lacked proper foundations in doctrine, structure, and handling church conflicts.

But along with church growth came unforeseen problems which were not understood at the time. Faulty organizational foundations were laid out of hastiness or ignorance. Churches functioned more as large centers of worship and teaching than covenant communities of committed believers. Church structure was deemphasized, and church discipline was down played.

Even with its failings, however, the Charismatic renewal reached and affected most societies in the world. The Church learned how to use the mass media to obtain impact, with a tremendous proliferation of broadcasting and publishing ministries. The 700 Club, P.T.L and Trinity Broadcasting Networks became established television ministries, hosting the trendiest teaching, news and personalities, and even a Christian soap opera. Many groups splintered over doctrinal and methodological questions, as so often happens in times of Church expansion. These developments had both positive and negative effects. Let us learn from the negative experiences as well as the positive, so we can serve our King and His Kingdom wisely.

WHY MOVEMENTS DIE

The fact that a true spiritual movement from God can die is no surprise to anyone who studies the Bible. The apostle Paul warned the Galatian churches:

Galatians 3:3,4. Are you so foolish? Having begun by the Spirit, are you now being perfected by the flesh?

The warning in Hebrews is even more explicit, drawing upon the example of the generation of Israel that perished in the wilderness through unbelief.

Hebrews 3:17-19. And with whom was He angry for forty years? Was it not with those who sinned, whose bodies fell in the wilderness? And to whom did He swear that they should not enter His rest, but to those who were disobedient? And so we see that they were not able to enter because of unbelief.

Christ's message to the Ephesian church, in the Book of Revelation, was equally stern. While He praises the church for great work and perseverance, He states:

Revelation 2:4,5. But I have this against you, that you have left your first love. Remember therefore from where you have fallen, and repent and do the deeds you did at first; or else I am coming to you and will remove your lampstand out of its place--unless you repent.

Movements can die for many reasons. A few of these are:

1. Practicing truth in a mechanical way (Matthew 23)
2. Following a method rather than the Spirit and the Word (Scripture examples: the brazen serpent in Numbers 21:9 and II Kings 18:4; the fall of Bethel, an early house of worship in Israel in Genesis 28:19 and Amos 4:4; Matthew 15:2-6; Mark 7:6-13; Colossians 2:8)
3. Making external expressions of truth, without internal changes (Matthew 23:1-7,23-28; Colossians 2:20-23)
4. Obedience without a heart of love--legalism (I Samuel

1:10-15)
5. Allowing place for a critical spirit in a movement
   (Proverbs 17:19; Matthew 12:24; Revelation 12:10)
6. Allowing people's involvement with a move of the
   Spirit to attach to a personality rather than a Bible
   truth (I Corinthians 3:4-9)
7. Allowing imbalance or overemphasis of truth
   (Proverbs 16:11 and 20:10 and 20:23; Matthew 23:24)
8. Allowing emphasis on one aspect of truth to cause a
   break in fellowship with other bodies (Ephesians 4:3;
   Philippians 2:1,2; I Corinthians 3:1-5 and Matthew
   12:22-30)
9. Emphasizing the gifts over the fruits that the gifts are
   intended to produce (Revelation 2:20-23; Galatians
   5:22; Matthew 7:15-20; Acts 8:17-23)
10. Having no vision for progressing into maturity
    (Proverbs 29:18)
11. Allowing spiritual pride (Deuteronomy 8:11-20;
    Proverbs 16:18)
12. Focusing on a truth more than on the Lord Jesus
    Christ (John 5:39)
13. Being conformed to the world system rather than to
    the Lord Jesus Christ (Revelation 3:14-18; Romans
    12:1,2; I John 2:16-17; Hebrews 10:1)

With this biblical foundation on spiritual movements
and the factors affecting them, let us move on to
understand the present spiritual condition of the Church
today especially in the English-speaking world.

4
Understanding Our Present Spiritual Condition

"We must hear clearly what the Spirit is saying so that the Church can walk on to maturity without giving way to extremes."

The movements of the Holy Spirit can be likened to waves that grow and grow, gaining momentum until they break on the seashore. Let's call this the *wave principle* of God's visitation.

God is the wavemaker. But sometimes when God does not make the wave according to our timing or taste, we try to create our own waves. You can see a man-made wave making machine at some recreational parks today, especially in the Midwest. There is no ocean nearby, so these parks produce waves for the wave seekers. What they produce looks like a real wave. It feels like a real wave. The park even sounds like the beach--noise, sand, laughter--but the sand is not the real beach and the water only produces artificial waves.

So it is in the Church today. Even though the wave of past visitations has broken upon the seashore of humanity and then recedes, many Christians are still trying to create the same sense of movement. They are human wavemakers who say the right words, play the right music, push all the right buttons and get the people to say, "The wave is moving!" and "We're on the wave again!" In spite of their best efforts, however, we must confess that the true wave cannot be made by man. It is time to assess what the waves of visitation have brought in and what our condition is now. Every wave moves out sooner or later. Let us illustrate this graphically on the next page.

The wave of visitation recedes and then the true spiritual condition of the church is revealed. Wise leaders will allow the Holy Spirit to expose the faulty foundations without becoming defensive or making excuses.

As the wave of visitation moves, it brings with it the specific truths that the Holy Spirit wishes to emphasize and the one most needed by the Church. But we are tempted to enjoy the thrill of discovering the truths, without doing the work of giving them roots in the practice of our faith. A Christian can sometimes enjoy the power of the Holy Spirit but not submit to the sovereign lordship of Christ. He can enjoy healing without serving the healer. The wave of Holy Spirit power that ushers in these truths recedes sooner or later, requiring us to claim the truths without revival-time excitement. Down to reality we must come: daily living, family relationships, personal habits, finances, commitment to the Kingdom, and involvement in a local church. Such activities do not provide us with the same adrenalin-rush of excitement as we had experienced at the height of the visitation. Instead, we find ourselves in need of the discipline of the steady plodder.

It is God who allows this to happen, and He who wants it that way. God made the wave to break and to recede. It was not the devil or man. After the wave passes, what we have left is a candid revelation of our true spiritual condition, along with the challenge to gratefully apply the new truths to everyday life. We might not like it, but we must face it. God will not let us ignore practical living by living on top of the wave all of the time. Why? Because it is His purpose to build His true people into a strong, spiritual building, using those who still serve Him in everyday life after the wave has broken.

TWELVE REALITIES
OF THE CHURCH IN TRANSITION

Wherever the wave of the spiritual visitation breaks and recedes, the Church may face the following twelve conditions:

Power	*Without*	Purity
Presence of God	*Without*	Penetration of Heart
Popularity of Ministries	*Without*	Depth of Ministry
People Growth	*Without*	True Discipleship
Benefits Offered	*Without*	The Cost of Benefits
Leaders Promoted	*Without*	Preparation or Testing
Anointing Accepted	*Without*	Proving of Character
Church Growth	*Without*	Church Health
Promises Claimed	*Without*	Qualifying the Process
Worship Emphasis	*Without*	Doctrine to Balance or Establish Worship
Vision Overstated	*Without*	Biblical Substance or Wisdom
Trends Followed	*Without*	Holy Spirit or Clear Scriptural Leading

This list is a picture of what the Church faces after the passing of each spiritual visitation. The Church is in transition. Where is it going? We must hear clearly what the Spirit is saying so that the Church can walk on to maturity without giving way to extremes. The challenge faced by the modern Church is similar to the challenges laid before the Church in the Book of Revelation:

Revelation 2:7,11,29. He who has an ear, let him hear what the Spirit says to the churches. To him who overcomes, I will grant to eat of the tree of life, which is in the Paradise of God...He who overcomes shall not be hurt by the second death...Remember therefore what you have received and heard; and keep it, and repent. If therefore

you will not wake up, I will come like a thief, and you will
not know at what hour I will come upon you.

Seven obvious areas of change face the present
Church. We must identify them in order to find solutions
and lead the Church forward.

AREAS OF CHANGE	*PROBLEMS*
1. Church Structure	Confusion in leadership, eldership communication problems, disagreement over methods, senior or co-equal pastorships. Problems usually arrive when change comes too fast, with lack of foundational instruction.
2. Worship	Confusion, disagreement over new forms or methods of worship, conflict between new forms and older traditions. Opinionated people complain "it's not like it used to be" or "we stand too long" or "too many choruses, no hymns" or "need more depth."
3. Ministry	Confusion over who qualifies for ministry, job descriptions needed, priesthood of all believers taken to extremes, usurps governmental ministry; five-fold ministry taken to

extremes, the church becomes dormant. Clear teaching needed in this important area of ministry.

4. Family

Over-emphasis on family produces imbalance. Some teach: "put family before ministry, before the Church, almost before God." Balanced teaching needed: is family an extension of church, or is church an extension of family?

5. Character

Over-emphasis on character development can make Christians passive, inactive, with no motivation to serve the Church or witness for Christ. When personality blemishes become more important than bearing fruit, the Body of Christ becomes too limited.

6. Teaching

Over-emphasis on teaching produces a spiritually fat but unproductive church, and hinders outreach and relationships. When over-emphasized, the following areas of teaching produce the following imbalances:
• Character--no outreach;
• Bible Typology--no practical

                                    teaching;

- Spirituality--no doctrinal structure;
- Love--no standards of purity.

7. Relationship   Over-emphasis may cause an exclusive, closed fellowship, with small vision for outreach, missions, local church service.

The Church and the many transitions it has made is shown on the chart on the following page.

THE CHURCH IN TRANSITION			
Hebrews 12:26-28; Matthew 24:29; Ezekiel 37:7 Isaiah 21:19-21; Haggai 2:2-6, 21			
1st Coming ←			**2nd Coming** →
New Testament Church	**Dark Ages Church**	**Reformation Church**	**20th Century Church**
(33-100) *New Structure for new Church elders, deacons and saints.*	Change Confusion Conflict	(1400-1800) Reject Rome dominance. Local church finds new identity.	(1900-2000) Church structure redefined biblically.
Worship for all believers. Songs, hymns, spiritual songs.	Formalism Ritualism	Reject formalism. Priesthood of all believers.	Restored biblical worship with spontaneous praise.

THE CHURCH IN TRANSITION

Hebrews 12:26-28; Matthew 24:29; Ezekiel 37:7
Isaiah 21:19-21; Haggai 2:2-6, 21

1st Coming ←			2nd Coming →
Ministry a practice for all, not a position for few.	Concept change to professional	Laity restored to ministry function.	Identification of equippers and those being equipped. Ministry for all.
Family order taught to serve together in Kingdom of God.	Celibacy in the ministry. Family weakened	Priests marry. Family life re-emphasized	Family re-established as a Kingdom priority.
Character emphasized above charisma, fruit above gift.	World standards accepted in ministries and church.	New emphasis on sanctification and practical holiness	Legalism rejected. Biblical holiness defined and sought.

THE CHURCH IN TRANSITION			
Hebrews 12:26-28; Matthew 24:29; Ezekiel 37:7 Isaiah 21:19-21; Haggai 2:2-6, 21			
1st Coming ←			**2nd Coming** →
Teaching the practical and the theological.	Dictatorship Non-liveable theology	Bible expositors preach with new found understanding.	Bible preaching with new biblical scholarship.
Relationship	Professional	Spiritual	Church and Relationships

Transitions are part of Church life and bring needed changes. Here are four suggestions in handling transitions:

1. Develop convictions based on New Testament concepts and principles that apply easily to each of the seven areas of transition.

2. Maintain consistency of principles as change is needed, do not put emphasis on non-essentials or Church traditions.

3. Communication of biblical principles to the church continually will help the church focus on

the eternal Word of God and not cultural or traditional forms.

4. Learning how to go through the transitional times with wisdom and patience will allow God to shake out all that needs to be removed.

The areas of change and the problem areas that need balance in the Church today are those that only the Holy Spirit can fully and effectively address. As we prepare to put the House of the Lord in order, we must first solve multiple problems. This releases the Church to hear the Lord clearly and carry out His will in all wisdom. In the next chapter, we will begin to address the Church's leadership needs, and narrow our focus on the desperately needed Jeremiah ministries.

5

Understanding Our Leadership Dilemma

"God must raise up leaders who are willing to be enlarged and stretched into something new, relevant, and powerful."

In every level of society, from the family to the White House, America is suffering from a leadership vacuum. Fathers are no longer leading their families. Power-conscious politicians have replaced principled statesmen of the past. People are asking for strong, credible leadership they can follow. The Kingdom of God today also lacks credible, wise, and anointed leadership. It would be inaccurate to say the Church has no good leadership, but it definitely does not have enough. As the wave of visitation recedes and the Church faces its obvious problems, we now need wise leadership to guide the Church. The Church needs fathers in the faith, who understand the times, to arise and assume leadership.

These fathers could be called apostles and prophets of the Church. As the Lord brings forth true fathers, some counterfeits will also initially appear, because the work of man always runs ahead of the work of God. The Church desperately needs true apostles with God-proven ministries and proven wisdom in leading the Church. Their ministry is similar to the ministry of the apostle Paul, who described himself this way:

> *I Corinthians 4:15.* For if you were to have countless tutors in Christ, yet you would not have many fathers; for in Christ Jesus I became your father through the gospel.

Apostles have the ability to give the Church roots. They can tell us where we have been and what we should be building upon. Prophets can tell the Church where she should be going, giving the Church direction in a time of darkness and confusion. Apostles and prophets are two of the most needed ministries today. God provides five governmental ministries to the Church altogether: "He gave some apostles, and some prophets, and some as evangelists, and some as pastors and teachers...for the equipping of the saints...." (Ephesians 4:11,12).

Without true apostolic direction, the Church will fall victim to leaders who experiment with the sales potential of new teaching fads without providing true spiritual leadership in and through the Word of God. This is especially harmful to the Church when she must go through a time of rebuilding foundations and casting off chaff. A true apostle would build a model church that would prove to be effective in society today. On the bookshelves of our Christian bookstores and churches, we have more than enough books on church planting and church growth strategies. What we need are proven churches!

Isaiah prophesies about the leadership lack in Israel and the devastating consequences. The full context of Isaiah 3:1-12 should be read. Let us quote and remark on just a few thoughts from this prophecy which seem to be fitting for the Twenty-First Century Church. In Isaiah 3:1 the prophet states that God is going to remove from Jerusalem and Judah both supply and support, the whole supply of bread and the whole supply of water and...

Isaiah 3:2	"The mighty men"
3:2	"The women"
3:2	"The judge"
3:2	"The prophet"
3:2	"The diviner"
3:2	"The elder"
3:3	"The captain of fifty"
3:3	"The honorable man"
3:3	"The counselor"
3:3	"The expert artisan"
3:3	"The skillful enchanter"
3:4	"I will make lads their princes"
3:4	"Capricious children will rule over Them"
3:5	"The people will be oppressed"

This indeed is a bleak picture of what the Lord intends to do to a people who "rebelled against His glorious presence." (Isaiah 3:8) The nation became leaderless. No mighty men, no warrior to put courage in the hearts of the would-be warrior. No true prophet to trumpet truth without fear of reputation, reward, or life itself. No honorable leaders of integrity who would model truth, honesty, and character. No counselors who would counsel by the principles of God's Word.

The result is heart breaking--a nation whose

leadership is childish and weak.

> *Isaiah 3:12.* "O My people! Their oppressors are children, and women rule over them. O My people! Those who guide you lead you astray and confuse the direction of your paths."

Could this be a clear picture of our present dilemma? Could the problem of a leaderless Church be the result of uncorrected sin and unrepented wrong doing?

Isaiah states the problem very clearly:

> *Isaiah 51:18,20.* There is none to guide her among all the sons she has borne; nor is there one to take her by the hand among all the sons she has reared...Your sons have fainted, they lie helpless at the head of every street like an antelope in a net, full of the wrath of the Lord, the rebuke of your God.

What a devastating prophecy! Those who were born in Israel, those who should have been able to lead, were not equipped to do so. A whole generation of 'sons', and not one prepared to be a *father.*

Isaiah laments that Israel has "none to guide her, none to take her by the hand." A guide who takes another by the hand is someone who cuts a new trail that others can follow. Spiritual trailblazing is a far cry from the scenic tour guides we so often get instead as leaders. We need leaders who will take us where we should go, not just ones who tell us about the loveliness of the trail! Isaiah lists several specific causes of such a lack of leadership. We will highlight two of them: fainting and entanglements.

First, Isaiah states that the "sons have fainted." To faint means to lose heart, to give up, to fall short of a goal. What applies here to the sons can apply in our day to the fathers. Church leadership needs a second wind, a fresh strength. Apostolic leadership seems weary, with so many involvements, so many committees, conventions and activities. The energy of the fathers must be redirected toward raising up leadership for a new generation. Is this what our leadership is so busy doing? Or are they wasting their strength on the wrong things? We should remember...

Proverbs 24:10. If you faint in the day of adversity your strength is small.

Galatians 6:9. We shall reap if we faint not.

Secondly, Isaiah states that the sons are "as wild antelopes in the net." The more furiously an animal kicks while entangled, the more tangled it becomes, until it wastes all its energy in the effort. What happens to the sons are consequences of what happens to the fathers. Could it be that those who should be apostolic and prophetic to the Church today are tangled up in church administration and business? What nets have tangled the cutting-edge leadership of the modern Church? Could it be the nets of self-ambition, pride, rivalry, and competition? Has Satan tangled leadership up with their own drives and weaknesses? God is looking for leaders who will surrender all to His Lordship--surrender their security, goals, ambitions, pulpits, church staff, ideas, their own "little kingdoms," and let Him cut the binding nets from off their lives and ministries. But the question still remains: Are we really willing to be untangled? What about our ministry status and our reputation? What about our building programs, our retirement centers, our control and ownership of the vision? Where are the true fathers? Are they going to model a new leadership that goes against the typical American success story?

God must raise up leaders who are willing to be enlarged and stretched into something new, relevant, and powerful.

Isaiah 50:4-6. The bed is too short to stretch on, the blanket too narrow to wrap.

To paraphrase, the Holy Spirit is telling us that we cannot wrap ourselves in the blanket of yesterday, or sleep in the bed of yesterday's ministry. God must raise up leadership that has an ear to hear what God is saying today (Isaiah 50:4-6). God must raise up leaders who will become voices of the present, not echoes of the past (John 1:23; I Corinthians 11:23; Galatians 1:12; I Corinthians 4:7). God must be the one who does all of these things--and we must cooperate with Him as He does!

If we do not cooperate with God, both the present fathers and the future sons will be too tired and overstressed to be able to lead the Church effectively. If we do not embrace this new direction, God will be forced, out of necessity, to go outside of the traditional training camps and religious orders to find fresh leadership for His people. This is exactly what God did in His raising up the ministry of John the Baptist. John was not found among the Jewish priests, scribes or rabbis, but God found and used him in the wilderness! Where did Jesus find His future leadership? Where will God find His future leadership for the Church of tomorrow?

6

Our Present Need: Jeremiah Leadership

*"A prophetic leader interprets and applies truth
in a way relevant to his generation."*

Along with the freeing of true apostles and prophets,
a new kind of leadership must also emerge. The present
spiritual condition of the Church and the present leadership vacuum cries out for it. The Church needs
prophetic leaders.

The Book of Jeremiah, which provides many prophetic insights to the Church today, also instructs us in the
ministry of the prophetic leader. Constructed from
several passages in Jeremiah, our definition is as follows:

> *The Prophetic Leader is a leader with Holy Spirit insight into God's purposes for his own generation. Possessing a shepherd's heart of wisdom, the prophetic leader leads the flock of God into His purposes without hype, without over-driving the sheep, without being caught up in trends or spiritual fads. The prophetic leader speaks out the truth of God clearly and faithfully, does not accommodate people with watered-down words, and restores the disillusioned sheep.*

Jeremiah was a true prophetic leader. He accurately describes his dual ministry of pastor and prophet in Jeremiah 1:1-19 (the prophet) and 23:1-40 (the shepherd/pastor). These two ministries combine to produce a unique spiritual chemistry with divine authority to meet the needs of today's Church. A prophetic leader speaks for the Lord. By divine appointment, a prophetic leader interprets and applies truth in a way relevant to his generation. A prophetic leader has insight into the moving of God in history.

JEREMIAH, OUR MODEL

Jeremiah tells us that his father was a priest in Anathoth, the land of Benjamin (Jeremiah 1:1). Although he was born into the priestly family, God called Jeremiah to the prophetic ministry (1:5). Over forty-one years he faithfully ministered to the house of Judah. He suffered rejection, persecution, slanderous lies and cruel torture as a result of his uncompromising prophetic word to Judah. He spoke truth to God's sheep as a faithful shepherd.

Jeremiah describes several important elements in his call as a prophetic leader:

> *Jeremiah 1:4-10.* Now the word of the Lord came to me saying, "Before I formed you in the womb I knew you, and before you were born I consecrated you; I have appointed you a prophet to the nation." Then I said, "Alas, Lord God! Behold, I do not know how to speak, because I am a youth." But the Lord said to me, "Do not say 'I am a youth,' because everywhere I send you, you shall go, and all that I command you, you shall speak. Do not be afraid of them, for I am with you to deliver you," declares the Lord. Then the Lord stretched out His hand and touched my mouth, and the Lord said to me, "Behold, I have put My words in your mouth. See, I have appointed you this day over the nations and over the kingdoms, to pluck up and to break down, to destroy and to overthrow, to build and to plant."

God accomplishes His work through seemingly inadequate workers, that the glory may belong to God and not man. God chooses and uses instruments rejected by man. He calls them and then sovereignly prepares, qualifies, and gives them His own message to speak. Jeremiah was this kind of an instrument.

All prophetic leaders need a similar divine commission, with a deep-rooted conviction that their call to this ministry is God-ordained. A sense of divine destiny must reside in the heart of this kind of leadership. Prophetic leaders need the Lord's Spirit to touch their lips with fresh, new, relevant, penetrating words to speak. These words must be bathed in God's divine authority and delivered with divine boldness in the face of all opposition. Prophetic leaders receive divine insight into the root problems of God's Church, not just the surface symptoms. This kind of prophetic clarity is doubly needed in the Church and society of our times, because this generation is in a time of prophetic obscurity.

Jeremiah was set by God's hand as a solitary beacon on a lofty tower, in a dark night, by a stormy sea, lashed by waves and winds, but never shaken from his sure foundation. His gentle nature was yielding, tender-hearted, affectionate, deep in love and commitment to God's people. To show the balance in his ministry, let us run a parallel comparison between the ministries of prophet and pastor.

PROPHETIC LEADERS	**PASTORAL**
Jeremiah 1:1-19; Ezekiel 3:17, 33:7; I Samuel 9:9	Jeremiah 23:1-20; 25:34-38; 31:10 and 50:6-7
1. Prophetic calling certain	1. Pastoral calling to wounded sheep
2. Prophetic perspective clear	2. Pastoral patience toward unresponsive sheep
3. Prophetic insight proven	3. Pastoral discernment of false shepherds
4. Prophetic warnings faithful	4. Pastoral intercession for scattered sheep
5. Prophetic burden shouldered	5. Pastoral wisdom in feeding sheep
6. Prophetic hope repeated	6. Pastoral accountability for each sheep
7. Prophetic truth without compromise	7. Pastoral integrity
8. Prophetic motivation without hype	8. Pastoral heart maintained

The need today is so clear. God, give us leaders who have a shepherd's heart and a prophet's words! As prophetic leaders begin to minister faithfully, they must face all temptation with an overcoming spirit, because they will be tempted to proclaim only as much of God's word as the people will receive without rejecting God and the prophetic ministry.

God warned Jeremiah what would happen if he failed to resist this temptation--judgment would come upon the messenger as well as the people (1:17). Every leader of the Church is tempted to preach exclusively on popular themes with words that please the hearers. It is far more difficult to preach penetrating, prophetic messages that challenge the hearts of every hearer to change and embrace God's ways. But we must preach the threats with the promises, the judgments with the blessings, the rebukes with the condolences!

We will always be tempted to *adapt* the message of God to the constantly declining values and convictions of society around us. But we cannot afford to compromise God's truth to His people. Prophetic leaders must rise in the midst of spiritual lukewarmness and speak *hot* words from God that will shake the Church and cause her to become what she was called to be.

Let us receive the admonition, as well as the promise, that God gave to Jeremiah:

> *Jeremiah 1:12.* You have seen well, for I am watching over My word to perform it.

7

Biblical Understanding of Divine Warnings

"While the prophets and preachers have a responsibility to warn God's people, all of God's people have a corresponding responsibility to heed the warning."

Jeremiah uttered prophetic warnings to Judah for forty-one years without any sign of genuine repentance in the nation. They were facing the greatest crisis of their lives and yet they did not know it. Though he remained faithful to the last (Jewish legend has it that he died a horrible death for speaking the word of the Lord), Jeremiah's frustration showed.

Jeremiah 6:10. To whom will I speak and give warning, that they may hear? Behold, their ears are closed, and they cannot listen. Behold, the word of the Lord has become a reproach to them; they have no delight in it.

Does Jeremiah sound like anyone you know--perhaps

yourself? Most of the leaders of the Church in the past have made similar statements. Now again the Church is as Judah was then. We will look back on the last half of the 20th century as a pivotal era in the history of the Church.

Never in such a short time have individuals and nations experienced such radical restructuring in every area of life: social, political, technological, financial, educational, and of course, spiritual. The American society that once was the symbol of excellence has now fallen to mediocrity in most areas.

People live in the constant fear of nuclear holocaust. When a major magazine recently surveyed high school students about their expectations of the future, the most common response was, "What future?!" The teens understand that a few angry terrorists or renegade governments could easily cause worldwide havoc, perhaps even spark a nuclear war. Violence is already epidemic in several regions of the globe, and seemingly incurable.

All this confusion is not just overseas in somebody else's backyard. Terrorism in the U.S. takes a high-tech twist in computer viruses that are carefully engineered to produce shutdowns, loss of data, and malfunction in tens of thousands of networked computers. After one recent national incident involving an especially damaging virus, the U.S. Department of Defense was quick to claim that a virus could not infect their high-security systems. We must not be lulled into rejecting the possibility that some satanically-motivated individual could find a way to access *the button* that launches the arsenal of a nuclear arms country, thus precipitating a true nuclear holocaust!

The vaunted American industrial might appears to be crumbling. Countries like Japan, which is only one percent Christian, are outcompeting America in its own domestic market, as well as worldwide. The Japanese have become the new exemplar of excellence in their products, their economy, and their stable family life. What is wrong with *Christian* America? The American family structure is falling apart, with an alarmingly growing rate of single-parent and dysfunctional families. America has done exactly what Judah did 2500 years ago. The nation has forsaken the God of the Bible and replaced Him with many modern idols, among them materialism, pleasure, sex, and entertainment.

> *Jeremiah 2:11-13.* "Has a nation *changed* gods, when they were not gods? But My people have *changed* their glory for that which does not profit. Be appalled, O heavens, at this, and shudder, be very desolate," declares the Lord. "For my people have committed two evils: they have *forsaken* Me, the fountain of living waters, to hew for themselves cisterns, broken cisterns, that can hold no water."

> *Jeremiah 2:20-24.* "For long ago I broke your yoke and tore off your bonds; but you said, 'I will not serve!' For on every high hill and under every green tree you have lain down as a harlot. Yet I planted you a choice vine, a completely faithful seed. How then have you turned yourself before Me into the degenerate shoots of a foreign vine? Although you wash yourself with lye and use much soap, the stain of your iniquity is before Me," declares the Lord God. "How can you say, 'I am not defiled, I have not gone after the Baals?' Look at your way in the valley! Know what you have done! You are a swift young camel entangling her ways, a wild donkey accustomed to the wilderness, that sniffs the wind in her passion. In the time of her heat who can turn her away? All who seek her will not become weary; in her month they will find her."

Where is the Church during this *megatrend* change in our society? We are living in a time of the global restructuring of life. Values are changing rapidly, sometimes with no more reason than personal whim. Humanism is the new worldwide cultural consensus. The New Age philosophy has seeped into our music, art and schools.

Where is the Church? In other times, an average society's values would change over a period of fifty or one hundred years. Now every decade, values are being challenged, redefined and taught differently. Genetic engineering is raising questions about the moral capacity of man. Interplanetary travel is on the horizon. A new pill that induces abortions was pushed through by the French government, against religious opposition; and it may hit the American market soon--no doctors needed for an abortion now, no appointments in a clinic with the attendant risks and shame--just a convenient, personalized murder in the privacy of the individual's own home. With this pill, the fetus dies within twenty-four hours. Our senseless medical industry maintains the life of the elderly in a medical crisis long past any reasonable point-- heroic yet futile efforts which seem to reflect strong respect for the sanctity of life. Yet, when hospitals accidentally fail to kill late-term fetuses in *botched abortions,* or when a child with massive birth defects is born, our medical industry no longer rules out the option of infanticide; and the murdered child's body may be sold to the cosmetic or medical research industry.

Are we dwelling on negatives a little too much here? Is all of this a little too heavy-spirited? Let us ask a more important question: where is the Church during these incredible changes in our society?

The Church, by and large, is lagging far behind in addressing the dilemmas of our modern society. She seems to still be struggling with archaic problems and questions over doctrine, church structure, and methods. This indicates that the Church is satisfied with its present condition, with no real passion for change. Her attitude is, "Give me my job security, my retirement, my home and family, and do not bother me." It is so easy to think our future is secure when it is not. The rotten foundations of our society will not bear up under the weight of much more corruption, greed, and debt. Our security is false. Our only security is in turning to God in true repentance and building on godly, biblical foundations in our families, our churches, and in our society. When all the shaking is finished, the Kingdom of God will still be standing as strong as ever.

With such strong similarities between Jeremiah's Judah and today's world, Jeremiah's warnings are very current and very important for Christians today. But before we state the many warning signs for the Church today which are based on Jeremiah's ministry, we must fully understand the purpose, seriousness, and nature of any kind of biblical warning:

> *Hebrews 12:25-28.* See to it that you do not refuse Him who is speaking. For if those did not escape when they refused him who warned them on earth (Moses), much less shall we escape who turn away from Him who warns from heaven. And His voice shook the earth then, but now He has promised, saying, 'Yet once more I will shake not only the earth, but also the heaven.' And this expression, 'Yet once more,' denotes the removing of those things which can be shaken, as of created things, in order that those things which cannot be shaken may remain. Therefore, since we receive a kingdom which cannot be shaken, let us show gratitude, by which we may offer to God an acceptable service with reverence and awe.

TAKE HEED TO THE WARNING OF GOD

A warning does not imply *business as usual.* One

might infer from this fact that warnings to God's people would be relatively rare. Unfortunately, both the fallen nature of the world around us and our own sinful state create inevitable conflict between God and His people, making frequent warnings necessary. Both in the Old Testament and the New Testament, warnings are common.

Old Testament

The Hebrew word for warning carries the meanings *to gleam, to enlighten by caution, to admonish.* The law itself was both a light and a warning to God's people:

> *Psalm 119:105a.* Your word is a lamp unto my feet.

> *Psalm 19:11.* Moreover, by them *(God's laws, statutes and judgments)* Your servant is warned; in keeping them there is great reward.

The Old Testament prophets were given to Israel by God so they could warn them by applying the Law through the Spirit in specific situations. Warning was at the very heart of Ezekiel's commission from God:

> *Ezekiel 3:17.* "Son of man, I have appointed you a watchman to the house of Israel; whenever you hear a word from My mouth, warn them from Me."

In this office of prophetic watchman, he would answer with his own life if he failed to speak out God's warning--as forcefully as a trumpet--of approaching judgment (Ezekiel 33:1-9). Jeremiah, too, understood that warning must be a primary function for him:

> *Jeremiah 6:10.* To whom shall I speak and give warning, that they may hear? Behold, their ears are closed, and they cannot listen.

80

New Testament

The New Testament Greek word for warning carries the meanings *to put in the mind, to caution or reprove gently, to call attention to.* The apostle Paul, the standard-bearer for missionary zeal in the New Testament, also understood warning as one of his primary responsibilities. Even as he actively developed the theology of justification by faith, he actively warned God's people against their own sins.

> *Acts 20:31.* Therefore be on the alert, remembering that night and day for a period of three years I did not cease to admonish (KJV *warn*) each one with tears.

> *I Corinthians 4:14.* I do not write these things to shame you, but to admonish (KJV *warn*) you as my beloved children.

> *Colossians 1:28.* And we proclaim Him, admonishing (KJV *warning*) and teaching every man with all wisdom, that we may present every man complete in Christ.

EXHORTATIONS TO TAKE HEED

In both the Old and New Testaments, the words for *take heed* have the meaning of directing the mind toward something, and taking actions as a precaution against something. While the prophets and preachers have a responsibility to warn God's people, all of God's people have a corresponding responsibility to heed the warning.

In chapter three of the Book of Hebrews, we have a set of areas in which to heed the warnings of God, based on the wilderness experience of Israel before entering the promised land. This passage explains that we will likewise enter a *promised land* of covenant rest in Christ--but only if we heed the warnings of God, just as Israel was tested and required to heed. In what we can call *wilderness warnings*, the Church must take heed to the Lord in the areas of:

- A hearing ear (3:7)
- A hardened heart (3:8)
- Testing the Lord (3:9)
- An errant heart (3:10)
- Knowledge of the Lord's ways (3:10)
- The evil heart of unbelief (3:12,18,19)
- Exhortation one to another (3:13)
- Deception by sin (3:13)
- Steadfast confidence in Christ (3:14)

Scripture is filled with exhortations to take heed, to be mindful of what the Law and the Spirit say regarding many areas of our faith and walk. We are exhorted to take heed:

- To ourselves (I Timothy 4:16; Hebrews 3:12)
- To our ways (Psalm 39:1)
- To our spirits (Malachi 2:15,16)
- To the leaven of religiosity (Matthew 16:6; Mark 8:15)
- That no man deceive us (Matthew 24:4; Mark 13:5; Luke 21:8)
- To watch and pray (Mark 13:33)
- To how we hear (Luke 8:18)
- To what we hear (Mark 4:24)
- To what lightens our spiritual understanding (Luke 11:35)
- To avoid covetousness (Luke 12:15)
- To the condition of the flock of God (Acts 20:28)
- To how we build (I Corinthians 3:10)

- To how we use our liberty (I Corinthians 8:10)
- Lest we fall (I Corinthians 10:12)
- That we not consume one another (Galatians 5:15)
- To the ministry we have received (Colossians 4:17)

With these exhortations to heed what God reveals, let us apply an open mind and an earnest heart to the warning signs to the Church today.

8

Red Alert Signal #1 for the Church Today

*"People are too busy to apply what they hear.
Their lives are out of control."*

RED ALERT SIGNAL #1

*When a people no longer have prophetic ears to hear
prophetic truth.*

One of the key words in the Book of Jeremiah is the
word *listen,* along with its synonyms. The meaning in the
Hebrew word is *to perceive a message, to give attention, to
hear effectively and critically, to hear with understanding so as
to result in obedience.*

The call to hear God involves more than just thought
or feeling responses. It requires knowing clearly what He
is saying, grasping the meaning of what He is saying, and
responding by putting God's word into practice. Hearing
God involves understanding, and understanding requires

reshaping one's whole perception of the meaning of life. Only when a word from God is allowed to reshape perception and activity will it produce a harvest of righteousness over an extended period of time.

Not to listen intently to God's voice through His written word and spoken word is to commit spiritual suicide. Over and over again we read in Jeremiah that Judah refused to hear and obey. They heard, but refused to respond, and the outcome was seventy years of captivity in Babylon. The Church must develop a hearing heart. This is probably the most critical need today because it affects every other area of Church life.

> *Jeremiah 11:10.* They have turned back to the iniquities of their ancestors who refused to hear My words, and they have gone after other gods to serve them.

> *Jeremiah 13:10.* This wicked people, who refuse to listen to My words, who walk in the stubbornness of their hearts and have gone after other gods to serve them.

(For similar verses, see also Jeremiah 6:10,17 and 7:13,27 and 16:12 and 17:24,27 and 18:19 and 26:3-5 and 25:13 and 37:2 and 28:15 and 44:16; Ezekiel 3:7-9.)

> *Proverbs 28:9.* He who turns away his ear from listening to the law, even his prayer is an abomination.

> *Amos 8:11.* "Behold, days are coming," declares the Lord God, "when I will send a famine on the land, not a famine for bread or a thirst for water, but rather for hearing the words of the Lord."

> *Proverbs 8:34.* Blessed is the man who listens to me, watching daily at my gates, waiting at my doorposts.

In practice, spiritual hearing problems have not one

but *several* roots and expressions. To deal with the problem effectively, we need to outline some of the more common roots.

Itching Ears.

This speaks of people who will not stand healthy, balanced teaching. They will search for and find teachers who will satisfy their own personal drives and lusts. They want their ears *tickled* with whatever sounds good and is presently acceptable to them.

Teachers who pander to their lust (it is an easy way to fill a church) will turn away from the reality of the Scripture and begin to say only what *sells*. Even legitimate ministries in the Word can cultivate an ability to push the right button to get an emotional response from the audience; and when they do, they are bordering on ministerial hype and emotional manipulation.

People in the Church today have had their ears tickled so much that it takes an absolute *expert* to tickle their ears now. Tricks, jokes, stories and drama, when applied in the wrong spirit, can all fit into the strategy of tickling ears.

> *II Timothy 4:3.* For the time will come when they will not endure sound doctrine; but wanting to have their ears tickled, they will accumulate for themselves teachers in accordance to their own desires.

Uncircumcised Ears.

This hearing problem is caused by a backslidden heart that needs renewal and reviving. It is like a field that has been plowed but was neglected too long, causing it to become hard. This field will not yield any crop because the soil is too hard to receive any seed.

> *Jeremiah 4:3,4.* For thus says the Lord to the men of Judah
> and Jerusalem, "Break up your fallow ground, and do not
> sow among thorns. Circumcise yourselves to the Lord and
> remove the foreskins of your heart, men of Judah and
> inhabitants of Jerusalem, lest My wrath go forth like fire
> and burn with none to quench it, because of the evil of
> your deeds."

Stubbornness of Hearing.

This is a problem of rebellion, self-will and stiffened necks. The heart is the root of all hearing problems. Self-will and willfulness always results when the heart is not receiving anything fresh from the Holy Spirit. Maybe a person is afraid of losing a truth if he hears it balanced with another one. Maybe a Christian simply does not want to hear, perhaps out of fear of being convicted of sin. Whatever the motivation, stubbornness of hearing comes from a stubborn heart.

> *Zechariah 7:11,12.* But they refused to pay attention, and
> turned a stubborn shoulder and stopped their ears from
> hearing. And they made their hearts like flint so that they
> could not hear the law and the words which the Lord of
> hosts had sent by His Spirit through the former prophets;
> therefore great wrath came from the Lord of hosts.

Dullness of Hearing.

To be dull of hearing is to be slow, sluggish, and shallow of heart. The sending station is in order, but the receiving station is out. Hebrews 5:11 implies that people who are keen of hearing can nonetheless fall into this condition. This happens when people begin to become calloused--they hear but do not obey, creating a separation and a distance between themselves and God.

> *Hebrews 5:11.* Concerning him we have much to say, and it is hard to explain, since you have become dull of hearing.

Forgetful Hearing.

This is a common hearing problem in today's Church. The Word is preached but not embraced with obedient hearts. People are too busy to apply what they hear. Their lives are out of control. This condition is like that of the one who looks in a mirror and sees what he needs to change, but as soon as he leaves the mirror he forgets. James labels this as a self-deception that leads to dead religion.

> *James 1:17,22-25.* Every good thing bestowed and every perfect gift is from above, coming down from the Father of lights, with whom there is no variation, or shifting shadow...But prove yourselves doers of the word, and not merely hearers who delude themselves. For if anyone is a hearer of the word and not a doer, he is like a man who looks at his natural face in a mirror; for once he has looked at himself and gone away, he has immediately forgotten what kind of person he was. But one who looks intently at the perfect law, the law of liberty, and abides by it, not having become a forgetful hearer but an effectual doer, this man shall be blessed in what he does.

Faithless Hearing.

To hear the Word and not mix it with a living faith is to profit nothing. The Word preached to Israel in the wilderness did not profit them because of their unbelief. This illustrates the power of unbelief, doubt and negative thinking. God's Word did its utmost to accomplish God's work, constantly beating upon their ears so as to enter their hearts by faith, but they were hardened. Faithless hearing can negate the Word of God in every generation.

This prophetic warning sign must be taken seriously, and an immediate remedy sought. If the Church continues to neglect God's voice, God will find ways to get her attention. We need to dig the spiritual wax out of our ears and turn them daily to the Lord through Holy Spirit-inspired prayer and study in the Word.

Luke 1:38. And Mary said, "Behold, the bondslave of the Lord; be it done to me according to your word." And the angel departed from her.

Isaiah 50:4,5. The Lord God has given Me the tongue of disciples, that I may know how to sustain the weary one with a word. He awakens Me morning by morning, He awakens My ear to listen as a disciple. The Lord God has opened My ear; and I was not disobedient, nor did I turn back.

9
Red Alert Signals #2 and #3 for the Church Today

"Rottenness in the Church is sometimes well hidden and disguised."

RED ALERT SIGNAL #2

When a people refuse to discern the depth of their spiritual decay and rottenness.

How can we diagnose the health of the Church today? May I suggest it's not by comparison with one another, or by comparison of different churches or ministries. Health can only be examined by comparing ourselves with the Word of God--not culture, not society, not what the educational system says is right or moral, but what the Lord has said.

Rottenness happens when a people who were clean have become unclean, and their uncleanness becomes worse than their original uncleanness before salvation.

Rottenness is in evidence when the Church judges sin by the standards of the world. The people of God display rottenness when they dress, talk, live and think like the sinful elements in the society around them. A society that is humanistic, rejects godly values, exalts self-centeredness and glories in decadence is not to be emulated by the godly.

Rottenness in the Church is sometimes well hidden and disguised. But rottenness cannot be hidden for long because it decays the house of God, allowing groaning and collapse when storms come. Refusing to face the depth of our spiritual rottenness in the Church today only delays our own disaster. We see all around us--in the Church, too--declining morality, disrespect for authority, glorification of individuality. The Church gives her blessing on her own forms of humanism, filling the Church with the same rottenness that is destroying the world system.

Chuck Colson states, "It strikes me that the prevalent characteristics of our culture today are rampant narcissism, materialism, and hedonism. Our culture passes itself off as Christian with 50 million Americans, according to George Gallup, claiming to be born again. But it is dominated almost entirely by relativism. The 'do your own thing' mind set has liberated us from the absolute structure of faith and belief and set us adrift in a sea of nothingness."

As the more Christian-dominated consensus weakens, the majority of people will adopt two impoverished values: personal peace and affluence.

Personal peace means just to be let alone, not to be troubled by the troubles of other people, whether across the world or across the city--to live one's life with minimal possibilities of being personally disturbed. Personal peace means wanting to have my personal life pattern undisturbed in my lifetime, regardless of what the result will be in the lifetimes of my children and grandchildren. Affluence means an overwhelming and ever-increasing prosperity--a life made up of things, things, and more things--a success judged by an ever higher level of material abundance.

The collapse of so many American families should warn the Church that she is going in the wrong way! The Church's acceptance of the spirit of rottenness is evident even to the world around us, through the toleration of immoral Church leadership. How much rottenness have we allowed in the Church? Too much! It is time to teach and implement biblical standards and biblical values.

> *Jeremiah 24:2,8.* One basket had very good figs, like first-ripe figs; and the other basket had very bad figs, which could not be eaten due to rottenness...."Like the bad figs which cannot be eaten due to rottenness--indeed, thus says the Lord--so I will abandon Zedekiah king of Judah and his officials, and the remnant of Jerusalem who remain in this land, and the ones who dwell in the land of Egypt.

RED ALERT SIGNAL #3

When a people do not learn from the mistakes and failures of past spiritual movements.

Jeremiah records that the Lord commanded him to go to the gate of the temple in Jerusalem and deliver an important word (Jeremiah 7). It was his purpose to address the root problem in Judah. Their attitude toward sin was perverted. They had deceived themselves into thinking that as long as they went to the temple and performed their religious ceremonies they would be all right. Jeremiah came to speak a prophetic word that would deliver them from their deception.

Jeremiah 7:3-11. Thus says the Lord of hosts, the God of Israel, "Amend your ways and your deeds, and I will let you dwell in this place. Do not trust in deceptive words, saying, 'This is the temple of the Lord, the temple of the Lord, the temple of the Lord.' For if you truly amend your ways and your deeds, if you truly practice justice between a man and his neighbor, if you do not oppress the alien, the orphan, or the widow, and do not shed innocent blood in this place, nor walk after other gods to your own ruin, then I will let you dwell in this place, in the land that I gave to your fathers forever and ever. Behold, you are trusting in deceptive words to no avail. Will you steal, murder, and commit adultery, and swear falsely, and offer sacrifices to Baal, and walk after other gods that you have not known, then come and stand before Me in this house, which is called by My name, and say, 'We are delivered!'-- that you may do all these abominations? Has this house, which is called by My name, become a den of robbers in your sight? Behold I, even I, have seen it," declares the Lord.

The Lord's word was to Judah: "How can you think that coming to My temple excuses you to commit abominations like murder?" And that word is still true today. How much innocent blood has been shed in America? Through abortion alone, a million Americans are murdered every year. We have hundreds of gods, too-- the new cars that we buff up every Saturday, the television altars that occupy hours of every day, and a list which goes on and on. We say to ourselves, "I am in church, in church, in church," and this, by itself, places us on good terms with God. The truth is that we need more than good church attendance to please Him.

Many in Pentecostal and Evangelical circles come to church on Sunday, and practice sin every other day. Christian people are viewing pornography, committing adultery, embezzling money--even in *innocent* ways like taking questionable tax write-offs. Many Christians are doing these things privately, then coming to church and saying, "But we're delivered!" God says, "No way!" But they say, "Oh yes, the sweetness of the temple of the Lord, the glory of worship. We're delivered from sin." Yes, but *delivered* only until the next time they want to sin.

God says, "You'll pay." But they keep sinning privately, and since nothing happens, they think they are getting away with it. But God's response is, "No, payday is coming!" God writes the check, and He is never late. He always pays...and we always reap what we have sown!

Do you want to know what God does to a people who use His name but become wicked? Jeremiah warned that He would cast them out, just as He cast out the people of Ephraim who committed wickedness. Their place of worship, Shiloh, became deserted. The same could happen to the temple in Jerusalem, Jeremiah warned, and it did. The same could happen to our churches today.

Do not deceive yourself, or anyone else, with foolish words. Do not use the *grace* of your church and think that you can continue to sin, commit adultery or fornication, or be a homosexual and sing in the church choir. Do not think that you can be a closet homosexual or lesbian and not *bother* anybody else; teach a Sunday school class but never touch or affect the children. Do not deceive yourself. Attending a house of God will not cover your sins. God will come down and will correct you, as He did Shiloh and Jerusalem. The temple at Jerusalem was restored, but only after that sinning generation was long gone. It was destroyed again after that.

Chuck Colson in his book, *The God of Stones and*

Spiders, sums up our philosophical delusion. He says, "20th Century wrath of God has been dismissed as the product of puritan prudency. Right and wrong are no longer moral absolutes to live by, but psychological hang-ups to be healed!"

10

Red Alert Signals #4 and #5 for the Church Today

"We are left to deal with our own hearts that so desperately want to believe convenient lies."

RED ALERT SIGNAL #4

When a people choose prophets based on their approval of the prophetic word without any interest in biblical accuracy.

How it must have wounded Jeremiah to watch Judah glorify a slick seller of snake oil like the prophet Hananiah. Jeremiah experienced only rejection for his faithful efforts to turn the hearts of Judah back to God, while Hananiah received a hero's welcome for telling people the lies that they wanted to believe.

Jeremiah 28:1-4. Hananiah the son of Azzur, the prophet, who was from Gibeon, spoke to me in the house of the

Lord in the presence of the priests and all the people, saying, "Thus says the Lord of hosts, the God of Israel,'I have broken the yoke of the king of Babylon. Within two years I am going to bring back to this place all the vessels of the Lord's house, which Nebuchadnezzar king of Babylon took away from this place and carried to Babylon. I am also going to bring back to this place Jeconiah the son of Jehoiakim, king of Judah, and all the exiles of Judah who went to Babylon,' declares the Lord,'for I will break the yoke of the king of Babylon.'"

Hananiah the prophet probably had a very charismatic ministry with a powerful delivery of his words. He prophesied a word that was very positive, very encouraging--and very false. God had no intention of bringing about the fulfillment of this prophecy, but doubtless the people were in absolute agreement and were overjoyed with Hananiah's word. The *Hananiah Factor* is relevant to our own day. Many Hananiahs move with strength of personality and self-made charisma, and prophesy what the people want to hear. They prosper because people will embrace false preaching and prophecy much more easily than the truth. Truth hurts sometimes. Truth demands changes. This kind of pain and inconvenience--who needs it? The answer: God's people do. Jeremiah brought a word of truth that cut right through Hananiah's self-serving prophecy.

Jeremiah 28:5-11. Then the prophet Jeremiah spoke to the prophet Hananiah in the presence of all the people who were standing in the house of the Lord, and the prophet Jeremiah said, "Amen! May the Lord do so; may the Lord confirm your words which you have prophesied to bring back the vessels of the Lord's house and all the exiles from Babylon to this place. Yet hear now this word which I am about to speak in your hearing and in the hearing of all the people! The prophets who were before me and before you from ancient times prophesied against many lands and against great kingdoms, of war and of calamity and of pestilence. The prophet who prophesies of peace, when the word of the prophet shall come to pass, then that prophet will be known as one whom the Lord has truly sent." Then Hananiah the prophet took the yoke from the neck of Jeremiah the prophet and broke it. And Hananiah spoke in the presence of all the people, saying, "Thus says the Lord, 'Even so will I break within two full years, the yoke of Nebuchadnezzar king of Babylon from the neck of all the nations.'" Then the prophet Jeremiah went his way.

People usually buy into the prophets that say what they themselves want to hear. As people approve of their prophecies, the prophet grows stronger and stronger in confidence. He says to himself, "Well, bless God, these people like me. They hear and enjoy what I am prophesying." There is a leadership principle in the Bible that God will give a people the kind of leadership that they deserve. In our own day, when people, for example, buy into the extreme prosperity syndrome, they will buy into all the people who preach sermons that support that fallacy. It is a self-perpetuating circle that takes false preachers and false or gullible Christians down the wrong road together.

Yet this kind of preacher is immensely popular. This is not to slight the popularity of godly and legitimate preachers, but to expose those who prosper by merely feeding the itching ears and the market for what people want to hear. A certain publisher recently produced a book predicting that the Lord would come back on a certain date--and had a best-seller on its hands. Maybe they lost some credibility when their bogus prediction fell through, but they made a lot of money in the meantime. It seems very possible that financial profit was all that the publisher had wanted in the first place.

But let us see what happens when preachers get a little more subtle in selling convenient "words from the Lord." Let us prophesy something most Christians could more easily believe: "The Lord is going to break the yoke of all the nations off of America; the country will have a trade surplus, balance the budget, become a net lender nation again and assume the position of the dominant world power it once held in the 50s and 60s." (Maybe it will even happen, but is this a biblical priority from the Lord that should be our primary focus?) Our Bible tells us clearly that the Kingdom of God is everlasting. Every other kingdom will fail, but God's Kingdom will endure forever. America--and this may come as a shock to some people--is not one and the same as the Kingdom of God! Only the Kingdom of God will last forever, as will the people who follow the King.

We know what happens to a people who do not follow God. We know that Judah went into captivity. But what became of Hananiah?

Jeremiah 28:12-17. And the word of the Lord came to Jeremiah, after Hananiah the prophet had broken the yoke from off the neck of the prophet Jeremiah, saying, "Go and speak to Hananiah, saying, Thus says the Lord, 'You have broken the yokes of wood, but you have made instead of them yokes of iron.' For thus says the Lord of hosts, the God of Israel, 'I have put a yoke of iron on the neck of all these nations, that they may serve Nebuchadnezzar king of Babylon; and they shall serve him. And I have also given him the beasts of the field.'" Then Jeremiah the prophet said to Hananiah the prophet, "Listen now, Hananiah, the Lord has not sent you, and you have made this people trust in a lie. Therefore thus says the Lord, 'Behold, I am about to remove you from the face of the earth. This year you are going to die, because you have counseled rebellion against the Lord.'" So Hananiah the prophet died in the same year in the seventh month.

The passing of Hananiah did not solve the problems of Judah; nor would the death of false teachers and preachers heal our own deficiencies in the Church today. We are left to deal with our own hearts that so desperately want to believe convenient lies. Look around at the Church, at your fellow Christians, at yourself. The best place for us to be is on our knees crying out to God in repentance, for the Body of Christ, to a great extent, is not what she makes herself appear to be.

RED ALERT SIGNAL #5

When a people trust in religious substitutes and forsake God himself, the fountain of true spiritual life.

The people of Judah committed two evils. First, they forsook God, withdrawing from His satisfying river of life. Second, they turned to man-made cisterns in His place. They forsook the true source of joy, fulfillment and purpose to turn toward broken cisterns.

> *Jeremiah 2:13.* For my people have committed two evils: They have forsaken Me, the fountain of living waters, to hew for themselves cisterns,broken cisterns that can hold no water.

Judah suffered from a mixed character, with elements as diverse as light and darkness in a perpetual struggle for control. Her distinguishing mark as a nation was insight into God through the covenant and the prophets. Yet Judah also showed herself false, fickle, sensual, cruel as most any other people.

Such evil can only be the result of a fundamental turning away from the living fountain to bend her wandering steps toward a cistern of her own making, a broken cistern which could not store water. Such manmade reservoirs cannot satisfy the longing for the true life of God to touch the hidden heart of man. They cannot speak new words of direction. Like any manmade thing, they will soon break, decay, and stink. Such is the history of man and of God's people who forsake their true Source.

What man-made religious cisterns has the present Church created and labeled as *God-made*? Let us identify them and cast them away! Have we forgotten how fresh and alive God's river of the Holy Spirit is to His Church? He is the living water, the living bread, indeed He is life itself. The simplicity of God's river can be lost among the complexity of man-made cisterns. Do we have so many buildings, lights, recording and amplification systems that we have possibly forsaken the fountain of the Holy Spirit? Could our worship be more entertainment than worship, and our singing more mood, emotion and driving rhythm than spiritual offering to God?

Cisterns can store water, but they cannot create water. Cisterns are not a source of life, they are only a place to hold what once was life. God did not turn His back on Judah--Judah deserted God! Instead of seeking joy in their God, they began to seek it in other objects. They found temporal substitutes that only satisfied for a short time. No matter how well the cistern is made, if water is poured into it, it will leak.

What has the Church given up in forsaking the fountain of God for attractive cisterns? Have we become the more intellectual, philosophical Church, and risked the shipwreck of our faith as the apostle Paul warned? (I Corinthians 1,2) Have we become more theatrical with drama, dance, music, and the arts, but lost the drama of serving Christ? Have we become more respectable and approved in our own society, at the risk of rejection by God? Let us return to the fountains of God in the Holy Spirit which are continually available to the Church.

> *John 7:37-39.* Now on the last day, the great day of the feast, Jesus stood and cried out, saying "If any man is thirsty, let him come to Me and drink. He who believes in Me, as the Scripture said, 'From his inner-most being shall flow rivers of living water.'" But this He spoke of the Spirit, whom those who believed in Him were to receive; for the Spirit was not yet given because Jesus was not yet glorified.

Let us return to the simplistic worship we see in the Bible, and seek the beauty of the Lord. Let us thirst after God with fasting and prayer conventions, instead of entertainment and big-name speaker conventions. Let us seek to touch the world with our missionaries, sent out with the blessing of the Church and with adequate financing, instead of wasting funds on our own cisterns. If we repent, we can be the Church that Jesus said He would build.

> *Lamentations 3:40-51.* Let us examine and probe our ways, and let us return to the Lord. We lift up our heart and hands toward God in heaven; we have transgressed and rebelled, Thou hast not pardoned. Thou hast covered Thyself with anger and pursued us; Thou hast slain and hast not spared. Thou hast covered Thyself with a cloud so that no prayer can pass through. Mere offscouring and refuse Thou hast made us in the midst of the peoples. All our enemies have opened their mouths against us. Panic and pitfall have befallen us, devastation and destruction; my eyes run down with streams of water because of the destruction of the daughter of my people. My eyes pour down unceasingly, without stopping, until the Lord looks down and sees from heaven. My eyes bring pain to my soul because of all the daughters of my city.

GOD'S PEOPLE TRIUMPHANT IN PERILOUS TIMES

II Chronicles 7:14. And if my people who are called by My name humble themselves and pray, and seek My face and turn from their wicked ways, then I will hear from heaven, will forgive their sin, and will heal their land.

11

Red Alert Signal #6 for the Church Today

"Yes, God is love, but love must be balanced with justice and charity with holiness."

RED ALERT SIGNAL #6

When people build their spiritual house without righteousness and excuse themselves on the basis of comparisons to the culture around them.

So many Christians stumble into this condition without knowing it. It happens in degrees. Remember when you were first saved? If someone had told you that, in a few short years, you or some dear Christian friend of yours would again be behaving as the world around you, you probably would have responded, "Not me! No way! I'm going to be a light to the world!" Many of the Christians whose lives are no longer built on righteousness may have once said just that, at the beginning of their walk with Christ.

What happened? Does a Christian usually make one momentous decision one day, and then decide that the righteousness of Christ is without value? Usually not. Sin usually happens in degrees; but no matter: the final end of such a condition is just as bad as if they had decided in a moment to forsake holiness, maybe even worse.

> *II Peter 2:21-22.* For it would be better for them not to have known the way of righteousness, than having known it, to turn away from the holy commandment delivered to them. It has happened to them according to the true proverb, "A DOG RETURNS TO ITS OWN VOMIT," and, "a sow, after washing, returns to wallowing in the mire."

People cheat on their taxes--Christians!--and justify themselves with rationalizations about how rich people never pay taxes, therefore, why should they? Christians steal small (*inconsequential*) items or amounts from their employers, at the cost of their conscience. If they have the honesty to admit it, they would say that they were behaving as if they had never known Christ. It is as if they wanted all the good things that they thought God intended to give them, more than they wanted God Himself or His ways.

From there they continue going downhill. They decide that it is normal to have certain desires, that they should have whatever they desire, and that God isn't a parsimonious, unfriendly or legalistic sort who watches everything you do. Little by little, they edge away from God and become ruled by the base passions that have ruled the pagan spirit since Cain was born. "Other things are more important than holiness and righteousness. I do not need righteousness. I can still cheat, steal, lie, gossip, lust, and covet. It will not hurt me because I am just being human, and everyone is doing it."

Christian leaders have been too afraid to speak out against sin in the Church. For one reason, pastors can be sued for excommunicating associate pastors; and even excommunicated members have taken legal action against their pastors. Suddenly excommunication is not so popular, when a pastor rebukes people for sin and reaps only confusion in legal problems and pressure.

Some people in the Church have begun to see sin as unredeemed sinners themselves see it. They rationalize, "Surely God would not *want* to come down heavy on anyone for personal sin, would He?" They refuse to see that God is not the universal teddy bear just looking for someone to hug. Yes, God is love, but love must be balanced with justice, and charity with holiness. The same God who told Joshua, "Kill everybody in that city" is the same God we praise every Sunday for His loving-kindness. It is out of His love for us, that He will not tolerate sin in our lives. He knows, better than we do, that sin will destroy us.

Proverbs 30:12. There is a kind who is pure in his own eyes, yet is not washed from his filthiness.

Jeremiah 22:13. Woe to him who builds his house without righteousness and his upper rooms without justice, who uses his neighbor's services without pay and does not give him his wages.

II Peter 2:7-9. And if He rescued righteous Lot, oppressed by the sensual conduct of unprincipled men (for by what he saw and heard that righteous man, while living among them, felt his righteous soul tormented day after day with their lawless deeds), then the Lord knows how to rescue the godly from temptation, and to keep the unrighteous under punishment for the day of judgment.

107

Romans 14:17. For the kingdom of God is not eating and drinking, but righteousness and peace and joy in the Holy Spirit.

"When a nation, a society, a culture, or a civilization rejects God and worships the human mind and body,it is destined to self-destruct."

RED ALERT SIGN #7

When people trust various techniques, methods, philosophies, programs, and themselves more than God.

Whatever we trust in, we also build upon and tend to like. Whatever we lean on can take us closer to God or further away from Him, especially over the years.

Before we fully develop this concept and its consequences, we need to make a brief footnote about healthy, biblical self-image. The Bible clearly states that we are to love our own selves (Matthew 19:19; James 2:8). In doing so, however, we are not to glorify ourselves above our fellow man or above God. God is to be honored above all.

Philippians 2:5-7. Have this attitude in yourselves which was also in Christ Jesus, who, although He existed in the form of God, did not regard equality with God a thing to be grasped, but emptied Himself, taking the form of a bond-servant, *and* being made in the likeness of men.

I Peter 5b,6. You younger men, likewise, be subject to your elders; and all of you, clothe yourselves with humility toward one another, for God is opposed to the proud, but gives grace to the humble. Humble yourselves, therefore, under the mighty hand of God, that He might exalt you at the proper time.

We could mention numerous influences in our modern, humanistic society that encourage us to place man above God. Let us discuss one of the most pernicious--the New Age movement. New Age philosophy is an eclectic cluster of borrowed values from Hinduism, humanism, and the human potential movement that have been brought together into a loose coalition as an anti-Christian religion.

In Hinduism, God is not separate from or beyond the created order of things. God is in all and accessible to all people merely by looking within themselves. The Hindus have more gods than people, making their concept of the godhead so fractured and fragmented that it implied that a person must be his own god. Western humanism, ever resistant to a moral and personal accountability to God, has so easily latched onto this Hindu world view because it serves as a most convenient avenue of individualism. The New Age has a lot of devotees; and it shows up in many seemingly innocuous forms.

You may have learned from reading magazines or newspapers, or watching television, of the growing influence the New Age movement is having in public schools and other educational settings. New Agers cannot teach their beliefs in school as an offshoot of Hinduism, because that would involve promoting religion. Instead, they have developed a non-religious jargon that does not raise any immediate alarms to many people; and the Eastern influence is still coming through. Your own teenager, for example, may come home from school and spark the following conversation:

"Hey, Dad, do you know what I did today?"

"What did you do today, Son?"

"I centered."

"You centered? Did you score?"

"No, no, Dad. Not basketball. I was centering. I had a transpersonal experience at school."

"You what?"

"Yeah, I was visualizing how my inner self needs to be released with more power and creativity."

"Well, Son, that sounds real good that you are getting in touch with yourself."

Without even knowing it, you have just encouraged your son down the wrong path!

We must understand that the New Age and other humanistic philosophies are encouraging people to trust in themselves to the exclusion of all else. They start out saying, "Man is inherently good," which is a clear heresy against the biblical truth of the inherent evil of man (Romans 3:23; 5:8; 6:22-23). It is only one step more to say, "Whatever you choose to do is totally good."

With such a step, the New Agers have actually trained a person to reject personal accountability to God and to their fellow man, to reject the need for repentance, and to reject even the very idea of guilt and the all-important functions of the conscience. A moral relativism has replaced the Judeo-Christian ethic.

Do you know what New Agers say about Christianity? They say it is a slaughterhouse religion, a blood religion, a religion always telling people how awful they are. Christianity supposedly talks only about sin and hell, the devil, spiritual darkness, and how terrible the world is.

To anyone who does not truly understand Christianity, thoughts like this sound pretty believable. To them it may seem that preachers are always telling somebody to repent about something. They preclude that the concept of repentance is just an old fundamentalist tradition, handed down with a lot of other archaic, ignorant, and now-forgotten folklore.

Furthermore, after the New Agers have converted someone, they persuade him that the Church of Jesus Christ is simply an out-dated institution because of her primitive desires to *spank* you (in a spiritual sense), and always wanting you to feel bad about yourself. The New Age Movement is perceived as a coming savior to deliver mankind from all of Christianity's repressive guilt trips. Instead of recognizing the place for legitimate guilt, the movement simply says, "You are all right. You just need to find your real self and be released from all else that binds you." This seems very attractive to many people. After all, who does not instinctively *want* to feel free within himself?

Finding one's "real self" (or more accurately, the self that people would *like* to believe they are!) does not lead to salvation according to the Bible. It does not give a person an eternal foundation. The illusion gives only temporary and superficial improvements in personality, if it improves anything at all.

The New Age's denial of sin, guilt, and responsibility to God fails to reach to the root of man's problems: alienation from God. The Bible helps us here--even if we initially do not like what it has to say. The Bible clearly states that all of us are sinners, born into sin, and shaped in iniquity. But the Bible does not stop there at the point of guilt. It gives us God's solution to the problem: We need the blood of Jesus Christ to cleanse us from sin and place in us the eternal value that God sees in us.

When your teenager comes home and says, "You know, Dad and Mom, your values are fine for you, but I have to discover my own values," do not just praise his honesty. Do not be so eager to avoid antagonizing your child that you say, "Yes, Son, we understand that everyone needs to discover their own values. After all, God must become personal to you as He is to me." Your child has just signaled that he needs your help, and he probably realizes this need--otherwise he would not have said anything. So sit down, talk, and find out what your precious gift of God is truly thinking.

We must be spiritually alert and constantly in the Word to recognize and to refute the New Age movement. If we do not live according to the real thing--the Word of God--everyday, then our eyes will grow too dull to detect any serious threat.

Jeremiah 17:5-8. Thus says the Lord, "Cursed is the man who trusts in mankind and makes flesh his strength, and whose heart turns away from the Lord. For he will be like a bush in the desert and will not see when prosperity comes, but will live in stony wastes in the wilderness, a land of salt without inhabitant. Blessed is the man who trusts in the Lord and whose trust is the Lord. For he will be like a tree planted by the water, that extends its roots by a stream and will not fear when the heat comes; but its leaves will be green, and it will not be anxious in a year of drought nor cease to yield fruit."

Jeremiah 39:18. "For I will certainly rescue you, and you will not fall by the sword; but you will have your own life as booty, because you have trusted in Me," declares the Lord.

113

When a nation, a society, a culture, or a civilization rejects God and worships the human mind and body, it is destined to self-destruct. The Church in the First Century faced the ungodly humanistic philosophy of Greece, "Man is the measure of all things; man, not the gods; the relative not the absolute."

The human body was idolized. The human mind became supreme. Reason itself was worshiped. The Greeks search for knowledge was unending. Their probing produced a pantheon of skeptics, cynics, stoics, and epicureans. Their attempt to integrate bodily ills and the psyche was the beginning of psychiatry.

As it was then, so it is now. We face almost the same culture as the First Century Church. The culture we face today may be described as follows:

- A culture that dethrones God and deifies man's achievements.
- A culture that exalts human reason as supreme.
- A culture that trusts education and science to solve its problems.
- A culture that believes man is evolving into perfection.
- A culture that replaces God's moral absolute standards with situational ethics.
- A culture that promotes sexual pleasure and instant gratification.
- A culture that strives for a world utopia of prosperity and peace.
- A culture that makes the state the sovereign dictator over everyone.

We now face a culture which is basically humanistic with a relativistic approach to life. The absolutes of God's Word have been removed and now we suffer its awesome consequences. Fredrick More Vinson, the great former Chief Justice (1890-1953) saw clearly the problem. He states, "Nothing is more certain in modern society than the principle that there are no absolutes, all is relative, all is experience, the only absolute allowed is the absolute insistence that there is no absolute!"

13

Red Alert Signal #8 for the Church Today

"The Church is the only institution, outside of the family, that is called to minister to a Christian's spirit."

WARNING SIGN #8

When people allow a shallow commitment to and abuse of the Lord's day.

A Christian's church attendance can reflect his relationship with God. A Christian can try to say, "I love Jesus, the Head, but I do not love His Body, the Church." Relationship with God does not work this way. This thinking is unbiblical. To a great extent, you cannot separate the Head from the Body (See Matthew 25:40).

The local church should become a place where Christians go with expectation, commitment, consistent attendance, involvement, a desire to minister to others, along with an enjoyment of the place as a time of prayer, rejoicing, celebration, and hearing of God's Word. The corporate gatherings should renew the intensity of our spiritual lives so that we return to our neighborhoods and work places with a renewed faith, love, and zeal for Jesus Christ.

As a pastor, I hear a lot of different reasons to justify non-attendance. Some people argue that every day is the Lord's day, and not merely Sunday, so why make a great deal out of church attendance? In practical experience, I have observed that this attitude many times breaks down into a very shallow treatment of the Lord during all seven days of the week.

We do find that there is somewhat of a difference in the New Testament concerning the Old Testament sabbath (Romans 14:5,6) and the Lord's Day. Nevertheless, the corporate gatherings of the saints was strongly practiced and encouraged.

Acts 2:42. And they were continually devoting themselves to the apostles' teaching and to fellowship, to the breaking of bread and to prayer.

Hebrews 10:25. ...Not forsaking our own assembling together, as is the habit of some, but encouraging one another; and all the more, as you see the day drawing near.

The spirit of the law is not in the specific day, but in recognizing that whenever the Church gathers together there are many good and Scriptural reasons to be there.

Some people may see gathering on Sunday as inconvenient. I would ask them this question: Is their faith in Christ also inconvenient? At some point along the way, their faith in Christ will challenge them out of their own personal ease, but what will they do then,

forsake God? Sunday gathering is similar. It is a
personal investment with Scriptural purpose: to glorify
God, to thank Jesus, to strengthen others, to pray for
needs, to be instructed, to develop stronger relationships,
and to be renewed, so that we can all continue to grow as
Christians and gain new ground for Christ.

We need to remember that church attendance is only
part of a Sunday's activities. Sunday is a beautiful, God-
given opportunity to spend with our family, to return to
the simplicity and strength of prayer, reading the Word,
fellowshipping with people, worshiping, being renewed
in mind and spirit, and being revived in one's covenant
vows with God.

Let us pray that all humanistic attempts to secularize
Sunday will be stopped. I personally believe that the
only hope for America, outside of Christ, is for families to
return to treating the Church with respect. My own
family attends Church faithfully, and we consciously limit
our activities on Sunday. I practiced this long before I
became a pastor.

The Church is the only institution, outside of the
family, that is called to minister to a Christian's spirit. A
Christian is simply not going to receive that kind of
ministry at an organization such as the Elks, Moose, or
Odd Fellows. This is equally true with any racquetball,
soccer, softball, or little league club. The Church is called
to build you up in the most holy faith, but she needs your
cooperation, and she needs you to pitch in and give to
your fellow believers in ministering at your local church.

Jeremiah 17:19-22. Thus the Lord said to me, "Go and
stand in the public gate, through which the kings of Judah
come in and go out, as well as in all the gates of
Jerusalem; and say to them, 'Listen to the word of the
Lord, kings of Judah, and all Judah, and all inhabitants of

Jerusalem, who come in through these gates: thus says the Lord, "Take heed for yourselves, and do not carry any load on the sabbath day or bring anything in through the gates of Jerusalem. And you shall not bring a load out of your houses on the sabbath day nor do any work, but keep the sabbath day holy, as I commanded your forefathers."

14

Red Alert Signal #9 for the Church Today

"There still are Elmer Gantrys in the ministry, but thank God, not every pastor is money-hungry."

RED ALERT SIGNAL #9

When people are led by corrupted leaders who are motivated by pride, money and immorality.

When people are willing to follow corrupt leaders, they obviously do not put a top priority on following the Lord. They are headed for disaster but either refuse to believe it, simply do not care, or are totally ignorant of it.

Let us never confuse loving a fallen pastor and failing to discipline him properly. A fallen pastor needs discipline. He will profit from it personally, and his church will be less vulnerable to satanic attacks if this discipline is applied quickly, decisively, lovingly, and publicly. I know of one church in the states in which the senior pastor committed adultery with a woman in the church. When some other brethren came in and dealt with the situation, they recommended that the pastor take some time off, continue pastoring the church, and not tell the congregation about it!

Pride has been defined as *a high or inordinate [unduly favorable] opinion of one's own dignity, importance, merit, or superiority, whether as cherished in the mind or as displayed in bearing, conduct, etc.* Pride is taking too much pleasure or satisfaction in one's own accomplishments or in something *believed to reflect credit upon oneself.* Pride can be a false sense of self-exaltation and self-importance. In this sense, it is vainglory, i.e., an empty or unjustified pride.

Proverbs 25:14. He that boasts of a false gift is like clouds and wind without rain.

Pride is also *a lofty and often arrogant assumption of superiority in some respect.* There are some interesting synonyms for pride, too. Conceit: *implies an exaggerated estimate of one's own abilities or attainments, together with pride.* Egotism: *implies an excessive preoccupation with oneself or one's own concerns.* Vanity: *implies self-admiration and an excessive desire to be admired by others.* (The Random House Dictionary of the English Language, 1977.)

When God begins to use a person, especially in a large way, the temptation to pride enters when that person begins to attribute to himself or herself the credit (or "glory") for what God is really doing in and through them. For example, Paul had to rebuke the charismatic, though sensual Corinthians because they began to get proud over their use of spiritual gifts and forgot that God was the one who founded the Church in the first place and that, through the apostle Paul (I Corinthians 3:4-9; 4:6f). Paul asks them this piercing question,

> *Corinthians 4:7.* What do you have that you did not receive?

and similarly chimes John the Baptist, as well as James.

> *John 3:27.* A man can receive nothing except it be given to him from heaven.

> *James 1:17.* Every good thing bestowed and every perfect gift is from above, coming down from the Father of lights...

A preacher must always remember that it was Jesus who called and equipped him for ministry. Without deep brokenness, ministerial success can ruin a man of God. Therefore, take heart, if God is now stripping and breaking you, it is for His sovereign purpose and days of greater usefulness are up ahead. Remember what Jesus said in the vine analogy,

> *John 15:2* ...every branch that bears fruit, he prunes it, that it may bear more fruit.

Christians need to become concerned when ministers talk more about themselves than about Jesus, the Church, or the Gospel. God's will for every minister (whether TV evangelist or not) is to be accountable to his fellow elders. One reason why?: so that the moral and spiritual disasters that usually accompany pride may be averted.

Money has long been a snare of ministry. The sin is not that money is inherently evil, because it is not; the sin takes place when a minister's motives begin to be

123

centered around using his spiritual gifts for more than reasonably supporting his family. This is why Paul told Timothy in his first letter to his son in the faith that one of the character requirements of a bishop was a freedom from the love of money (3:3). Why? Because an inordinate greed for money is a root for all sorts of evils (6:10), promotes the occasion of many temptations (6:9) and can potentially lead away from the faith and into ruin and destruction (6:9f).

There still are *Elmer Gantrys* in the ministry, but thank God, not every pastor is money-hungry. To safeguard the proper stewardship over the money that God has given to us, we should send our tithe to the local church that we attend and expect the elders to properly handle the money through a thorough and accurate balance sheet in the annual business meeting.

Immorality is a snare that has taken down some of the greatest men of God who ever lived, David, in particular, and many throughout Church history. We all feel the terrible disappointment deep down in our spirit when we hear of another leader falling to immorality or financial scandal. We are not necessarily angry, but terribly disappointed and maybe a little discouraged.

People need to make sure that the leaders to whom they submit are also morally accountable to one another before the Lord. Men who are not morally accountable to other brethren are prime targets for the enemy.

In most cases, a minister who falls does not fall over-night. Usually, there is a series of inner, personal compromises in impure thoughts and habits and then small secret signs begin. Normally, an impure minister has neglected true prayer and fellowship with God in the Word for a long time. The Word and Spirit are no longer encouraged to cover and check his thoughts or his feelings. He probably is not seeking outside counsel and is beginning to be inwardly unfaithful to the marriage covenant with his wife. This is the practical advice of Proverbs 5 and 6 written in a time when prostitution and adultery were running rampant in Israel:

> *Proverbs 5:15-23.* Drink water from your own cistern, and fresh water from your own well. Should your springs be dispersed abroad, streams of water in the streets? Let them be yours alone, and not for strangers with you. Let your fountain be blessed, and rejoice in the wife of your youth. As a loving hind and a graceful doe, let her breasts satisfy you at all times; be exhilarated always with her love. For why should you, my son, be exhilarated with an adulteress, and embrace the bosom of a foreigner? For the ways of a man are before the eyes of the Lord, and He watches all his paths. His own iniquities will capture the wicked, and he will be held with the cords of his sin. He will die for lack of instruction, and in the greatness of his folly he will go astray.

> *Proverbs 6:23-35.* For the commandment is a lamp, and the teaching is light; and reproofs for discipline are the way of life, to keep you from the evil woman, from the smooth tongue of the adulteress. Do not desire her beauty in your heart, nor let her catch you with her eyelids. For on account of a harlot one is reduced to a loaf of bread, and an adulteress hunts for the precious life. Can a man take fire in his bosom, and his clothes not be burned? Or can a man walk on hot coals, and his feet not be scorched? So is the one who goes in to his neighbor's wife; whoever touches her will not go unpunished. Men do not despise a thief if he steals to satisfy himself when he is hungry; but when he is found, he must repay sevenfold; he must give all the substance of his house. The one who commits adultery with a woman is lacking sense; he who would destroy himself does it. Wounds and disgrace he will find, and his reproach will not be blotted out. For jealousy enrages a man, and he will not spare in the day of vengeance. He will not accept any ransom, nor will he be

content though you give many gifts.

The people of God should pray for their leaders as well as be aware of their moral and ethical standards. When ministers begin to use the Bible to justify immoral activities or think that they are somehow superior to the clear moral standards of the Bible, steps should be taken to confront these leaders because this is the smoke that usually indicates the fire of sin underneath.

Christians need to balance out the exhortation of Hebrew 13:17 which encourages them to submit to their leaders, and not take it to the extreme of blind, unthinking, and unbiblical obedience. The spirit of the Berean Christians needs to be in all believers, who Luke described as much more "noble-minded" than the Thessalonican Jews not only because they "received the word with great eagerness," but also because they were Scripturally-minded.

> *Acts 17:11.* ...examining the Scriptures daily, to see whether these things were so.

All of us, including leaders, must submit to the moral laws of the Word of God.

15

Red Alert Signal #10 for the Church Today

*"We know how dangerous idolatry is.
It is not a food that can be eaten in moderation."*

RED ALERT SIGNAL #10

*When people are consumed with idols of materialism,
sensuality and entertainment.*

Israel was overthrown in the wilderness long before
meeting the giants of Canaan. They were overthrown by
the wickedness of their own hearts, in succumbing to the
lure of idolatry. A whole generation died in the
wilderness because of it. Modern technology has changed
the way people worship idols today, but idolatry is still
very much alive and is still just as deadly.

In New Testament Greek, idolatry is the act of
worshiping something other than the true God. It means
fixing or focusing the heart upon something to love, or

127

having deep affection for something, more than for the true God. Idolatry is using the resources God has given to us to exalt something other than God and Jesus Christ.

In the Old Testament, idolatry was considered spiritual adultery. In the New Testament, covetousness is a form of idolatry (Colossians 3:5). Both idolatry and covetousness are the breaking of covenant with the Lord and the giving of avowed love to something or someone other than God. The Old Testament not only tells us that God prohibits idolatry in Isaiah 42, but also explains the main reasons why in Deuteronomy 11.

> *Isaiah 42:6-8.* "I am the Lord, I have called you in righteousness, I will also hold you by the hand and watch over you, and I will appoint you as a covenant to the people, as a light to the nations, to open blind eyes, to bring out prisoners from the dungeon, and those who dwell in darkness from the prison. I am the Lord, that is My name; I will not give My glory to another, nor My praise to graven images."

> *Deuteronomy 11:16, 26-28.* Beware, lest your heart be deceived and you turn away and serve other gods and worship them...See, I am setting before you today a blessing and a curse: the blessing, if you listen to the commandments of the Lord your God, which I am commanding you today; and the curse, if you do not listen to the commandments of the Lord your God, but turn aside from the way which I am commanding you today, by following other gods which you have not known.

Idolatry inherently stops God's plan to bless, exalt, and use His people as a source of blessing for all nations. Obviously, when God's people pursue other gods and are ravished by other loves, being such a blessing is impossible. God can only bless those with a true and loving heart toward Him.

In addition, idol worship always involved some form of sin that further degraded the worshipper--drunkenness, sexual immorality, or child murder. All of these sins are against God's covenant, contrary to His heart for His people, and opposite the very image of God that He has put into each one of us.

The New Testament does not negate the Old Testament prohibitions against idolatry in its uncovering of its spiritual roots. John writes:

I John 5:21. Little children, guard yourselves from idols.

Colossians 3:5. Therefore consider the members of your earthly body as dead to immorality, impurity, passion, evil desire and greed which amount to idolatry.

Idolatry is closely tied to covetousness. Covetousness is the greed or lust for a thing, experience, or power that is expected to give satisfaction, security or superiority outside of God or God's will. Hosea describes covetousness and idolatry at work together:

Hosea 4:7,12. The more they multiplied, the more they sinned against Me; I will change their glory into shame....My people consult their idol, and their diviner's wand informs them.

Idolatry is a passionate longing and pursuit of an evil desire, which sends a person running away from God, and leads him to build a substitute god in his own life. It may involve any number of immoral acts, but the spirit of idolatry is an unfaithful, wayward heart toward God.

Chuck Colson in his book, *The God of Stones and Spiders*, insightfully puts his finger on the cultural problem we face. He says, "A common thread runs through these images, the notion that life somehow gives us the right to have every whim and desire satisfied. Driven in the pursuit of pleasure, society has become miserable. The society we live in has developed a Disney philosophy. Disney is but a picture of the world at large which tends to exhaust itself on the mistaken notion that multiplying pleasures produces happiness."

The Bible tells us how to seek deliverance from idolatry, and it requires some work on our part.

First:
> *Colossians 3:2.* Set your mind (affection) on things above, not on the things that are on earth.

Second:
> *Matthew 6:19-21.* Do not lay up for yourselves treasures upon earth, where moth and rust destroy, and where thieves break in and steal. But lay up for yourselves treasures in heaven, where neither moth nor rust destroys, and where thieves do not break in or steal; for where your treasure is, there will your heart be also.

Third:
> *Matthew 6:33.* Seek first His kingdom and His righteousness; and all these things shall be added to you.

Fourth, follow the example of Peter:
> *Luke 18:28-30.* And Peter said, "Behold, we have left our own homes and followed You." And He said to them, "Truly I say to you, there is no one who has left house or wife or brothers or parents or children, for the sake of the kingdom of God, who shall not receive many times as much at this time and in the age to come, eternal life."

Fifth, receive God's seal of ownership and authority on your life:
> *Song of Solomon 8:6.* Put me like a seal over your heart, like a seal on your arm. For love is as strong as death,

jealousy is as severe as Sheol; its flashes are flashes of fire, the very flame of the Lord.

The best cure for spiritual idolatry is a deep, clear repentance and the building of a healthy foundation in Christ that leaves no room for idolatry. If a person finds himself in idolatry, the sooner he repents and the more forcefully he presses into a genuine commitment to Christ, the better off he will be. From studying the history of Israel, we know how dangerous idolatry is. It is not a food that can be eaten in moderation. It is a deadly poison that must be avoided altogether.

16

Red Alert Signal #11 for the Church Today

"We must model true Christianity for our children with our own lives and train them to follow after our example."

RED ALERT SIGNAL #11

When the youth of the godly become as the youth of the ungodly and still believe they are in covenant with God.

We have all been to some *Christian* youth group gatherings and wondered whether what was going on was really Christian. The music, the unstructured and fruitless activities, and the immorality that was tolerated made us question whether it was a Christian group. I have said to youth pastors who run this kind of program, "You are allowing your kids to live a lie. You are allowing them to think that by attending a church, they are okay with God." In such circumstances, they will actually be raised in a spiritual deception. Many of those kids have never been saved, and they have never even been challenged to face the issue of personal accountability to God. A program that strives for *relevance* may wind up casting off God's agenda and replacing it with the agenda of the current teen culture.

This problem has several causes, but the root cause of all is the spiritually-dysfunctional family. Too many Christian parents do not pursue a lifestyle of personal discipleship for themselves or for their children. Many families of troubled teens are not fully dedicated to God or to their local church. Do such parents think that they can send their children to a church youth group, while they personally undermine everything that their children are hearing at the group through their own uncommitted lifestyle, and still expect their sons and daughters to make any kind of a real commitment of faith to Jesus? It is highly unlikely.

Turning the Captivity of Youth

Satan is not waiting for Christian youth to graduate from high school or college before he attacks their faith in Christ. He is attacking their beliefs and godly character right now, with plans to enfeeble or destroy their walk with Christ before they can do any damage to the kingdom of darkness (Matthew 13:19). Satan has succeeded in setting four snares in the middle of our rebellious American youth culture: the sexual revolution, drugs, satanic music and the occult.

If you think taking candy from a baby raises a ruckus, wait until you find your kids involved in one of these snares! Getting your child *un-snared* is a giant contest of wills between you and your child (as well as his friends', the prevailing culture's, and Satan's). We have to take great care to prepare our children to avoid those snares in the first place. We must model true Christianity for our children with our own lives and train them to follow after our example. We must prepare them for spiritual warfare from an early age.

Youth Under Attack

Our children must understand that they cannot escape the necessity of spiritual warfare just because they are not yet adults. There are two kings, Jesus and Satan, just as there are two kingdoms, one of light and the other of darkness. The two do not mix.

> *Ephesians 6:12,13.* For our struggle is not against flesh and blood, but against the rulers, against the powers, against the world forces of this darkness, against the spiritual forces of wickedness in the heavenly places. Therefore, take up the full armor of God, that you may be able to resist in the evil day, and having done everything, to stand firm.

The descriptions and titles of the king of darkness reveal his character, and forewarn us about the nature of his attacks. Satan is called:

- Adversary, opponent, enemy
  (Job 1:6-12 and 2:1-7; Zechariah 3:1-7)
- Accuser, slanderer, whisperer
  (Matthew 4:1 and 13:39; John 8:44)
- Serpent, beguiler, enchanter
  (Genesis 3:1-4; II Corinthians 11:3; Revelation 12:9)
- Lucifer, light-bearer or deceiver
  (Isaiah 14:12; II Corinthians 11:13-15)
- Tempter, enticer, one who draws away
  (Matthew 4:3)

The work and activity of Satan are also clearly identified in the Bible:

- *seduce*: to mislead or deceive (I Timothy 4:1)
- *trouble*: to make afraid (I Samuel 16:14,15)
- *oppress*: to exercise dominion against, or to overburden (Acts 10:38)
- *vex*: to mob, to harass, molest, to cause to suffer at the hands of another, to afflict (Matthew 17:15)
- *bind*: to tie up, confine, fasten with cords (Luke 13:16)
- *possess*: to exercise power over, to control with a demon

Satan's Avenues of Attack
The following list will help us to prepare ourselves, as well as our children, against the enemy's attacks. Satan will attack our:

1. **Attitudes**--perspectives on life may be slanted toward unhealthy values, or putting a priority on unimportant things; teens may fall into the syndrome of boredom/dissatisfaction with everything, with no goals or motivation or zeal.
2. **Standards**--the laws by which we live (Isaiah 49:22; I Chronicles 17:17).
3. **Spirit** (II Corinthians 7:1).
4. **Relationships**--"I hate my parents" seems to be one of the rallying cries of youth; they may be reacting to hypocrisy, conflict, spiritual emptiness, argumentative atmosphere in the home; they may be developing a taste for unwholesome relationships, involving impure attitudes, sexual sin, or homosexuality. Kids seem to have a supernatural yearning for love, and

they'll go wherever they think they can get it.

5. **Thought life** (II Corinthians 10:3-5 and 11:3; Romans 12:1,2; Philippians 4:8,9; Matthew 16:22,23). Watching television can pile a terrific amount of cultural refuse into the mind of an undiscriminating youngster. It has been estimated that some kids have watched six years of TV by age 18. Heavy metal rock groups that promote sex and violence can create an addiction that takes kids 180 degrees away from worship, prayer and the *new song* that the Lord puts in our spirits. In adopting ungodly fashions, and arguing with parents on the subject, teens may be doing more than playing with clothes, they may be opening their self-image to the ungodly.

6. **Zeal** (II Corinthians 11:7; Revelation 3).

7. **Failures** (Romans 8:1,33,34).

8. **Self-worth**--despising self and so coming to despise our Maker opens the way to terrible, debilitating attacks. This kind of attack often paves the way for alcoholism and drug addiction.

9. **Goals**--every person needs sincere pursuit of a godly life, as held accountable by God-given personal goals. Satan wants people to have no goals, to cast off godly goals, or to adopt ungodly goals.

Turning the Captivity

Today is the day of deliverance for our youth. Do not put off deliverance from sin until the future. That just means you or your children do not really want it today. Ask, believe, and receive deliverance--today! The outworking of deliverance may take time, but deliverance can begin today, and there is no good reason for waiting. (Encouraging verses on deliverance are: Psalm 124:4-8 and 126:1-4; Proverbs 3:23-26; Isaiah 43:1,2 and 61:1,2; Luke 4:18,19; Hebrews 2:14.)

Fortunately, deliverance does not fail for a lack of help from God. He is always willing and always able. Deliverance depends on our cooperation, response to God, and willingness to obey Him.

Essential Steps of Deliverance
Follow these steps in response to the Holy Spirit and God will deliver you from your specific snare:

- Respond to God's grace.
- Recognize the exact point and area where you have been ensnared.
- Repent of all wrong that you have committed. Take personal responsibility for your actions.
- Receive forgiveness and freedom from the Lord. Claim a clean conscience through Christ's shed blood.
- Rise and walk in newness of life.
- Renew your commitment to the Lord and stay away from anything that may lead you back to the same snare.
(II Timothy 2:20,21 and John 11).

A Time of Offering Yourself
Today's youth are marked by a spirit of selfishness and self-centeredness. "I shall never die," seems to be the attitude. "There will always be more energy, more time, more resources to pursue important issues later; for now, let us do what we do best--play!" Christian teens can begin to develop a similar attitude in the thought, "If I destroy part of my life through sin, I can always give what is left over to God." This is not biblical thinking!

Yes, you can take your messed up, mangled, and devastated human life and humbly give it to the Lord, but there are some things that the Lord cannot fully restore: virginity, a missing limb, even sometimes impaired physical or mental faculties. It is better not to waste your life before you give it to the Lord. Give your all to Him now. Give Him the best of your life, and He will use that to His greater glory and to the building of His kingdom!

In the Old Testament, sacrifices offered on the altar were required by God's law to be young, healthy, and at the peak of their strength and development. They were to be tender, without blemish or scar, with no broken bones or diseases, and in no way disfigured. These young offerings truly ministered to God and helped all the believers lift their worship to Him, reminding them all that they were to give their best to Him! They were a sign of the true piety of the one offering the sacrifice. They were required by God--nothing else was acceptable.

Should we think this principle is no longer valid in the New Testament? Never! Romans 12:1 tells us to offer our bodies, and all that we are, as a living sacrifice to God! Great men of God in the Old Testament followed this principle.

Samuel served God as a priest in the temple at Shiloh from his youth, and heard and responded to God well before adulthood. He was the great religious leader who oversaw Israel's transition from the rule of judges into a united monarchy under David. (See I Samuel 1-3.)

Solomon made a personal covenant with God at the beginning of his reign. Because he desired wisdom to serve God rightly, God blessed Solomon with wisdom-- and with riches above all other kings. Solomon built and dedicated the great temple in Jerusalem, which was an occasion for all Israel to seek the Lord. (See II Chronicles 6:12-14; I Chronicles 22:5 and 29:1.)

Daniel purposed in his heart not to be defiled in captivity in Babylon. He maintained his integrity and purity in service to a pagan king. His ministry of prayer was one of the primary spiritual agents that God used in returning Judah to Jerusalem at the end of the Babylonian captivity (See Daniel 1,2,6,9).

Joseph, David and Josiah are three other great leaders in Israel's history who served the Lord from their youth up. (For Joseph, see Genesis 37-43; for David, I Samuel 17; for Josiah, II Chronicles 34:1-3.) Negative examples were Absalom, son of David, who murdered a sinful brother and rebelled against his father (II Samuel 15:10-12); and Rehoboam, the foolish son of Solomon who failed to understand the needs of Israel and forced a permanent split between the northern and southern kingdoms (II Chronicles 10:10-19).

Benefits of Being a Young Offering
- The tenderness of a young offering makes him ideally suited to the necessary shaping and molding by the hand of God.
- God protects a young offering, and spares it from disasters that would disqualify it from full service in the future.
- The young offering learns to take control of his or her life and make wise decisions that pave the way for a life of fruitful service.
- The young offering is more flexible, and more easily learns to trust God to do works beyond his or her own strength.

Christian parents and church affiliation are no absolute guarantee of any relationship with God. Every person must make his or her own commitment to Christ, and personally maintain it. If Christian parents fail to raise a new generation of healthy Christians, the Church's service to God will be anemic, and crippled.

Christians are accountable to God to watch over their children, understand their spiritual condition, and do all in their power to raise them with godly standards.

17

Red Alert Signal #12 for the Church Today

"Now is the time to make a painfully honest assessment of where we are spiritually and morally."

RED ALERT SIGNAL #12

When people lose their godly heritage, refuse to face the reality of spiritual degeneration, and continue as if all is well.

This is the adult Christian's version of Warning Sign #11 for youth. The same problem can be found in adults: a simple denial of truth accompanied by a willingness to receive the benefits of righteousness, but an unwillingness to pay any of the costs. Underneath it all, there is a well-covered up spiritual and moral rottenness that everyone else except the rotten one can smell.

When kids are in this condition, we call them

unsaved, mixed-up, at risk; when adults are in this condition, we call them hypocrites of the worst kind. Christians in this condition want only one thing: self-justifying comforts. They do not want anything to rock their boat or shake their grand illusion. Phrases like, "The church is fine just as it is. Why are you so radical? Why do you keep bringing up all this talk about sin?" are constantly thought and spoken.

As a pastor, it is difficult to preach sermons that criticize lazy spirituality and personal sin in the Church. It is much more enjoyable to preach the sermons that say, "I can do all things through Christ who strengthens me," or "Christ loves you and accepts you just as you are." One scripture, however, continually haunts me. Jesus said:

> *Matthew 24:37.* As it was in the days of Noah, so shall it be in the days of the coming of the Son of Man. They were eating, drinking, marrying and giving in marriage until the day that Noah entered the ark and they did not understand until the flood came and took them all away!

They continued as if nothing would ever change. And it all changed in one day with only eight people making it safely onto the boat.

The Church, in America especially, is living as if nothing will ever change. Too many American Christians think they will always have their job, their car, their home, their children in Christian school, their favorite political party, and that their excellent decisions and investments will forever be secure. But we must remember something: It is God who is in charge of every nation and every people.

When any nation (including the U.S.A.) breaks the laws and principles of God, sooner or later He will judge that nation. Security cannot continue in the presence of sin. If the Church does not rise up now and be the salt and the light of the world (as Jesus charges us to be in Matthew 5:13-16), then God will have to get our attention and motivate us providentially.

How will He do it? Will he use an economic, social, or political crisis? The moral attention-getters are out there, but they do not seem to be making much of a dent in our complacency. The American family continues to fall apart, with a frightening growth in the proportion of single-parent families. AIDS only possibly may be controllable in a few years--but how many people will either be infected or die first? Meanwhile, other frightening new variations of venereal diseases continue to make their own advances. Gang warfare is expanding in the cities and spreading from major cities to smaller ones. The dollar value lacks strength, and America is the world's leading debtor nation.

We are obviously suffering for some reason, but people would rather look for physical reasons than spiritual ones. The Church has to face her spiritual problems first, if the rest of the country is to have a chance of responding to God. How many people are willing to step forward, admit their own guilt, and humble themselves before God? How many Christian leaders are willing to confront their own personal sin-- while an even more sinful world watches on with contempt and ridicule?

Let us all just look at our relationship with God and ask, "Is what I am thinking, doing, and saying in accordance with the Bible? Am I where I should be with God? Am I really doing any obvious damage to the kingdom of darkness? Am I really being salt and light to the world?" If I am not making any difference for Christ and righteousness, then what good am I being? What is the true purpose of my life?

We are here to know and to love and serve God. To love God means taking dominion over the devil. You cannot love God, sit back, and just let everything go to the devil. You need to wholeheartedly serve the kingdom of God and become actively involved in the spiritual warfare that is constantly raging all around us.

18

God's People Triumphant in Perilous Times

"The true Church in these perilous times is moving from impotence to influence."

In the midst of perilous times God's true Church will surface in splendor and glory. We must not become discouraged with the state of the Church worldwide. Remember, there is a Church within the church, just like there was an Israel within Israel. Not all who call themselves church are really the Church.

Matthew 16:18. ...And upon this rock I will build My church; and the gates of Hades shall not overpower it.

Romans 9:6-8. But it is not as though the word of God has failed. For they are not all Israel who are descended from Israel; neither are they all children because they are Abraham's descendants, but: "through Isaac your descendants will be named." That is, it is not the children of the flesh who are children of God, but the children of the promise are regarded as descendants.

The true Church in these last days will be the remnant people of God who have paid the price to become Church. I am not speaking of remnant as in small, but as in character distinctives which separate the true from the false Church.

The word remnant means *that which is left after the separation, the removal or destruction, a special kept people, protected.* (See Zephaniah 2:7,9; 3:13, Revelation 12:17; 19:21, Matthew 25:2-13.)

The people of God today must keep a hope before them--a hope of God's Church coming to maturity through all the trials and tests in these last days. A person can endure almost anything as long as he has hope, as long as he can believe there may come a change for the better. A person of hope can put up with starvation, deprivation, and constant hardship. He can accept harsh confinement and life with discomfort if there is hope.

Our hope is in the Bible's promise of a glorious Church without spot or wrinkle which will display the glory of God in this present darkness (See Ephesians 5:25-31.) Hope opens doors where despair closes them. Hope discovers what can be done instead of grumbling about what cannot be done. Hope draws its power from a deep trust in God and in His unchangeable Word. Hope regards all the present problems as opportunities for the Church to be the Church. Hope sets goals and is not frustrated by repeated difficulties and setbacks. Hope is what motivates the Church to push ahead when it would be easier to quit.

We are a people of hope! I believe the Church will not fade away and become irrelevant. Billy Graham warned us several years ago, "...if the Church does not meet its responsibilities in this generation, it may go into eclipse."

The Church may, as it now stands, be increasingly

irrelevant to the average man and must suffer a rebirth or face the inevitable consequence of being unable to survive in its present form. I believe in the words of Jesus. The Church cannot lose. It will change. It will succeed! It will not go into an eclipse, but will rise with greater splendor than ever.

Matthew 16:18
(NIV)...And the gates of Hades shall not overcome it.
(Philips)...And the powers of death will never have the power to destroy it.
(AMP)...And the gates of hades, the power of the infernal forces shall not overpower it, or be strong to its detriment or hold out against it.
(Berkley)...And the gates of hell shall not hold out against her.

See also Psalm 9:13, Proverbs 31:23, Isaiah 26:2; 38:10; 60:11,18; Lamentations 2:9

The Church will manifest God's glory to this darkened culture because it is Christ's Church. Man cannot destroy it or stop it even with all its manifest failures.

Haggai 2:7-9. "And I will shake all the nations; and they will come with the wealth of all nations; and I will fill this house with glory," says the Lord of hosts. "The silver is Mine, and the gold is Mine," declares the Lord of hosts. "The latter glory of this house will be greater than the former," says the Lord of hosts, "and in this place I shall give peace," declares the Lord of hosts."

Numbers 14:21. "Indeed as I live, all the earth will be filled with the glory of the Lord."

Isaiah 60:3. And nations will come to your light. And kings to the brightness of your rising.

149

Habakkuk 2:14. For the earth will be filled with the knowledge of the glory of the Lord, as the waters cover the sea.

The glory of God will shine through Christ's Church, God's last instrument to speak to the world prior to the second coming of Christ. The word glory speaks of our own influence in these perilous times. There are six Hebrew words used for glory.

- *Hader -*   *beautiful, excellent, majestic.*
- *Tohar -*   *purity, transparency.*
- *Sebhi -*   *denoting that which is prominent and conspicuous.*
- *Addereth -*   *Something broad, expanding, limitless, able to go beyond natural realms.*
- *Hodh -*   *grandeur, awesome, spectacular.*
- *Kabod -*   *weighty, to be noteworthy or impressive, to have reputation as a person in a high social position,like a king with wealth and authority, with power to act, to have spreading influence.*

Deuteronomy 28:13. And the Lord shall make you the head and not the tail, and you only shall be above, and you shall not be underneath, if you will listen to the commandments of the Lord your God, which I charge you today, to observe them carefully.

The true Church in these perilous times is moving from impotence to influence. The Church will become a people of great influence and persuasiveness, having the ability to affect society for good. The true Church will have the power to move people to a living hope in God because of the glory of God in the Church.

The true Church in these last days will set the pace, demand respect, and hold a high reputation. This is not just a positive approach to life. It is the revealed destiny of God's people. We are moving from *impotence* to *influence*. The impotent Church has been disabled, useless, helpless and exhausted. It has been crippled by carnal division and shallow leadership, causing the Church to collapse in power. But this is not the condition in which God will leave the Church. No! He is and forever will be reviving and restoring His Church. The Church may be like the sick man at the pool of Bethesda in need of a miracle. The same Christ who healed the sick man is the same Christ who will heal His Church. The Church may be likened to the man who was lame at the Gate Beautiful, waiting for his unforeseen miracle.

John 5:1-8. After these things there was a feast of the Jews; and Jesus went up to Jerusalem. Now there is in Jerusalem by the sheep gate a pool, which is called in Hebrew *Bethesda*, having five porticoes. In these lay a multitude of those who were sick, blind, lame, and withered, waiting for the moving of the waters; for an angel of the Lord went down at certain seasons into the pool, and stirred up the water; whoever then first, after the stirring up of the water, stepped in was made well from whatever disease with which he was afflicted. And a certain man was there who had been thirty-eight years in his sickness. When Jesus saw him lying there, and knew that he had already been a long time in that condition, He said to him, "Do you wish to get well?" The sick man answered Him, "Sir, I have no man to put me into the pool when the water is stirred up, but while I am coming, another steps down before me." Jesus said to him, "Arise, take up your pallet, and walk."

Acts 3:1-2, 6-8. Now Peter and John were going up to the temple at the ninth hour, the hour of prayer. And a certain man who had been lame from his mother's womb was being carried along, whom they used to set down every day at the gate of the temple which is called *Beautiful*, in order to beg alms of those who were entering the temple. But Peter said, "I do not possess silver and gold, but what I do have I give to you: In the name of Jesus Christ the Nazarene--walk!" And seizing him by the right hand, he raised him up; and immediately his feet and ankles were strengthened. And with a leap, he stood upright and began to walk; and he entered the temple with them, walking and leaping and praising God.

The Church is positioned at Bethesda waiting for the living Christ to speak His word, "Arise. Be thou made whole!" The Church is positioned at the gate *beautiful*, waiting for the apostolic word to challenge her to rise to her feet and be made glorious. God is committed to making the Church healthy, restoring her to full beauty and full strength.

Ephesians 3:10-11. In order that the manifest wisdom of God might now be made known through the church to the ruler and the authorities in the heavenly places. This was in accordance with the eternal purpose which He carried out in Christ Jesus our Lord.

Ephesians 3:21. To Him be glory in the church and in Christ Jesus throughout all generations forever and ever. Amen.

Colossians 1:18. He is also head of the body, the church; and He is the beginning, the first-born from the dead; so that He Himself might come to have first place in everything.

Colossians 1:27. To whom God willed to make known what is the riches of the glory of this mystery among the Gentiles, which is Christ in you, the hope of glory.

The triumphant Church in the coming 21st Century will face a different world with different challenges. We want to be in step with the future. We want to meet today's challenges and prepare for tomorrow's possibilities. Before us may lie the most important piece of time in the history of civilization and the Church. We are approaching the dawn of a new era, a period of stunning technological innovation, unprecedented economic and political surprises, and great changes in world culture. The future of the church has never looked better if you look from God's standpoint--a view from above. Christianity must be true to its character and purpose, yet meaningful to the people of any given time and place. The delicate key is to avoid diluting or distorting Christianity in the process of adapting it to a given culture.

Deuteronomy 32:29. Would that they were wise, that they understood this, that they would discern their future!

Here are just a few challenges the Church in perilous times will face:

1.   The Church must wrestle with a world mind set that is increasingly secular in nature, humanistic and modernized; open to old occult practices.

2.   The Church may have to deal with economical and political breakdown on an increasing scale world-wide that will cause people to experience deep fear and lack of trust in anything.

3.   The Church will minister to a world that

has by and large lost the traditional family look, and lost traditional family values. Many more singles and single parent households will surface. The pressures on the 21st Century family unit will be difficult.

4.   The Church will probably make many changes with its missions vision and philosophy in the next ten to twenty years. America and England will not be the Missionary Centers, but Africa and Asia will take over. The traditional missionary as seen in 1700's through the 1900's will probably still exist in the year 2000, but with many other new strategies and ministries.

5.   The Church will face a culture that is polytheistic and syncretistic in nature. Syncretism may be defined as the eclectic form of many religions. Adults will take the best facets of each religion and form a new blended religion. Already we see this happening with the eastern religions becoming more prolific and the robbing of certain appealing aspects of Christianity, thus making new and fascinating religions. It will become more and more of a challenge to the true Christian Church to establish the basic tenets of Christianity before people are seduced into these false religions. We are fast becoming a nation filled with many gods and many religions.

6.   The Church must fight hard to maintain the basic spiritual values and truth that people thirty to fifty years ago believed in easily. This will take more careful articulation in the pulpit and more biblical proof to establish firm convictions in the hearts of people. Trends suggest that the importance of religion in people's lives will continue its slow decline.

7.   The Church will be challenged to actually produce what she has promised in the areas of relationships, spiritual power over sin and demonic powers, healing and miracles, and deep unity of spirit. Society today is looking for churches that have philosophies and programs that respond to their felt needs through highly personalized and relevant messages. People are looking for that which is fresh and exciting yet credible and substantive.

8.   The Church will need to train its leadership at home. Seminaries and universities may become increasingly more irrelevant and anti-God with anti-Bible inspiration. This will necessitate thinking through what really prepares a leader (both clergy and laity) to meet the challenges of tomorrow.

9.   The Church will face an incredible hunger in the hearts of people for spiritual experiences and spiritual realities. We know this is found in Christ, but we must know how to minister Christ.

10.   The Church will face religious consumerism which will tempt the Church to direct its energies to satisfying the expectations of members as customers instead of accomplishing God's primary purpose--true maturity of Christ's Church, and reaching the world with the gospel. Society will become more self-centered, more materialistic, and more driven to play.

11.   The Church of the future will face an older America to which they must minister. Advances in health care, medicine, nutrition, and leisure technology have helped increase the average life expectancy to seventy-eight years. There are now more senior citizens in the United States than teenagers.

12.   The Church of the future will face a culture that has no deep seated respect for the local church. Local church loyalty will be even more fickle than it is presently. People will be committed to their idea of God and of serving God (which will become more and more of a private affair). The local church will need to fight hard against these trends if it desires to become an influence in the coming years.

Francis Schaeffer in his book, *Escape From Reason*, states, "We must realize that we are facing a rapidly changing historical situation, and if we are going to talk to people about the gospel we need to know what is the present ebb and flow of thought-forms. Unless we do this the unchangeable principles of Christianity will fall on deaf ears. And if we are going to reach the intellectuals and the workers, both groups need to do a great deal of heart-searching as to how we may speak what is eternal into a changing historical situation."

Yes, the coming years will have great doses of perilous pressures, but the Church will arise and face these challenges. Why? Because we are destined to win, destined as God's people to fulfill our God-given task. Yes, there will be numerous challenges, but with a fresh touch of the Holy Spirit available to God's people, no challenge will go unconquered!

Revelation 21:1-3. And I saw a new heaven and a new earth; for the first heaven and the first earth passed away, and there was no longer any sea. I saw the Holy City, the new Jerusalem, coming down out of heaven from God, made ready as a bride adorned for her husband. And I heard a loud voice from the throne saying, "Behold the tabernacle of God is among men, and He shall dwell among them, and they shall be His people, and God Himself shall be among them...

Revelation 21:9-11. And one of the seven angels who had the seven bowls full of the seven last plagues, came and spoke with me, saying, "Come here, I shall show you the bride, the wife of the Lamb." And he carried me away in the Spirit to a great and high mountain, and showed me the holy city, Jerusalem, coming down out of heaven from God, having the glory of God. Her brilliance was like a very costly stone, as a stone of crystal-clear jasper.